One Ball
of Wool

One Ball
of Wool

DK | Penguin Random House

Project designer Charlotte Johnson
Project editor Kathryn Meeker
Photographer Ruth Jenkinson
Art director Jane Ewart

Managing editor Penny Smith
Senior managing art editor Marianne Markham
Jacket designer Nicola Powling
Pre-production controller Tony Phipps
Production controller Ché Creasey
Creative technical support Adam Brackenbury
Creative director Jane Bull
Category publisher Mary Ling

First published in Great Britain in 2015 by
Dorling Kinderlsey Limited
80 Strand, London WC2R 0RL

Copyright © 2015 Dorling Kindersley Limited
A Penguin Random House Company
10 9 8 7 6 5 4 3 2 1
001- 274532-August/2015

A CIP catalogue record for this book is available from
the British Library
ISBN: 978-0-2411-9717-2

Printed and bound in China

All images © Dorling Kindersley Limited
For further information see: www.dkimages.com

A WORLD OF IDEAS:
SEE ALL THERE IS TO KNOW
www.dk.com

CONTENTS

TECHNIQUES

HAVE A BALL!

The needlecraft revolution is still going strong. It could be the satisfaction of making your own, unique woollen goods, or it could be the relaxation of sitting down in that moment of spare time, snatched after the daily commute, to work with the gorgeous wool you couldn't resist in the store. Whatever your reason, the patterns in this book are sure to find a special place in your life. They are modern, sometimes a bit wacky, and all of them use just one ball of wool. You can adapt any of them to suit your taste – simply choose a different colour or add a bit of embellishment. So grab a cup of tea, put on your favourite music, commandeer the comfiest spot in the house and enjoy – you deserve it.

Urban Bobble Beanie Page 26

WHAT IS
ONE BALL
OF WOOL?

WOOL COMES IN MANY different shapes and sizes, from small, 50 gram balls to huge ones – 500 grams (or larger). There's no need to confine your crafting to just spun fibres either; we've used rubber tubing and wire. Almost any flexible material can be worked with knitting needles or crochet hooks. Experiment, have fun, and let your creative spirit run wild!

Variegated wools change colour as your work them, so that you get a colourful project from just one ball.

Industrial Rubber Clutch Page 18

Sea Monster Teaser Page 64

The weight, or thickness, or a wool should also be considered. If substituting, use one with the same weight specified in your pattern and adjust the size of your needles or hook to get the correct tension.

Live Wire Cuff Bracelet Page 28

Honeycomb Infinity Scarf Page 14

PROJECTS

TOP TIP

When tacking the bottom edge, be sure to leave enough slack in your stitches so that the beanie will stretch to fit around your head. If your stitching is too tight you won't be able to put your hat on.

NEON BEANIE

LIGHT UP THE DAY, or night, in this simple, ribbed beanie hat. The hat fits snugly on the head with no slouch. If neon isn't your thing, you can choose any other DK weight yarn, just make sure you have enough length in the ball you choose. This pattern uses 170 metres (186 yards) of the specified ball of yarn. Make sure your ball has enough meterage if swapping.

YOU WILL NEED

Difficulty
Beginner

Size
To fit an adult female

Yarn
One ball of Stylecraft Double Knit Special; 100g; 295m (322yds); 100% acrylic. We've used colour 1257 Fiesta.

Knitting needles
One pair of 4mm (UK8/US6) needles

Notions
Blunt-ended yarn needle

Tension
22sts and 30 rows to 10cm (4in) over pattern on 4mm (UK8/US6) needles

HOW TO MAKE

Cast on 104sts using the cable cast-on method.
Row 1: [K2, p2] 26 times.
Rows 2 – 6: As row 1.
Row 7: P.
Row 8: [P2, k2] 26 times.
Rows 9–62: As row 8.
Row 63: P2 [(k2, p2) 4 times, k2, p2tog] 5 times, k2. (99sts)
Row 64: P2, [p2tog, p1, (k2, p2) 4 times] 5 times, k2. (94sts)
Row 65: P2, [(k2, p2) 4 times, k2tog] 5 times, k2. (89sts)
Row 66: P2, [k2tog, k1, (p2, k2) 3 times, p2] 5 times, k2. (84sts)
Row 67: P2, [(k2, p2) 3 times, k2, p2tog] 5 times, k2. (79sts)
Row 68: P2, [p2tog, p1, (k2, p2) 3 times] 5 times, k2. (74sts)
Row 69: P2, [(k2, p2) 3 times, k2tog] 5 times, k2. (69sts)
Row 70: P2, [k2tog, k1, (p2, k2) 2 times, p2] 5 times, k2. (64sts)
Row 71: P2, [(k2, p2) 2 times, k2, p2tog] 5 times, k2. (59sts)
Row 72: P2, [p2tog, p1, (k2, p2) 2 times] 5 times, k2. (54sts)
Row 73: P2, [(k2, p2) 2 times, k2tog] 5 times, k2. (49sts)
Row 74: P2, [k2tog, k1, p2, k2, p2] 5 times, k2. (44sts)
Row 75: P2, [k2, p2, k2, p2tog] 5 times, k2. (39sts)
Row 76: P2, [p2tog, p1, k2, p2] 5 times, k2. (34sts)
Row 77: P2, [k2, p2, k2tog] 5 times, k2. (29sts)
Row 78: P2, [k2tog, k1, p2] 5 times, k2. (24sts)
Row 79: [Sl1, k2tog, psso] 8 times.

Making up
Pass the yarn through the remaining eight stitches and leave a long end to sew up the side with a neat overcast stitch. The bottom six rows will naturally turn to the inside, so loosely tack these to the inside using a length of extra yarn, to make the edge look chunky.

HONEYCOMB INFINITY SCARF

THIS SCARF IS MADE using the "cheats" way of creating a Mobius strip, by creating a long scarf, twisting it, then joining the two ends together. You will be able to make three scarves using the recommended ball of yarn. Good news, as once everyone sees yours they will want one for themselves. There's everyone's birthday gifts sorted for the year!

YOU WILL NEED

Difficulty
Beginner

Size
Scarf measures approx 200cm (79in) in circumference

Yarn
One ball of Drops Verdi; 350g; 1,225m (1,340yds); 48% acrylic, 20% wool, 17% polyester, 15% mohair. We've used colour 08 Orange/Yellow/Brown.

Crochet hooks
7mm crochet hook
8mm crochet hook

Notions
1 stitch marker (SM)
Blunt-ended yarn needle

Tension
Tension is not important for this project, but as a guide 5 rows and 5 "V" sts to 10cm (4in) using a 7mm hook

Special abbreviations
Slip Stitch Join Sl St Jn
"V"Stitch 1tr, 1ch, 1tr in same place

HOW TO MAKE

Scarf
Using an 8mm hook loosely ch 26.
Row 1: Using a 7mm hook and ensuring that you work into the top loop only, miss 3 ch, "V" stitch in 4th ch from hook, *miss 1 ch, "V" stitch in next ch, rep from * to last 2 ch, miss 1 ch, 1tr in last ch. Turn. (11 "V" sts)
Rows 2–101: 2ch (counts as 1tr) * "V" stitch in 1ch sp, rep from * to end, 1tr in last ch. (11 "V" sts)
Do not fasten off.
Put a SM in the loop on the hook and remove hook.

Making up
Lay the scarf flat with row 1 at the top (with tail end to the left at the top and the marked loop at the bottom, also to the left). Bring the last row towards row 1, twisting the scarf, so that the marked loop is now on your right-hand side. Remove SM and replace with the 7mm hook.
Row 102: 1ch. Sl st to 24th ch of FC. *1tr in 1ch sp of "V" st in row below, Sl St Jn to ch at base of "V" st in row 1. 1tr in 1ch sp of "V" st in row below, rep from * to end.
Sl st to 1st ch made in FC.
Fasten off and sew in ends.

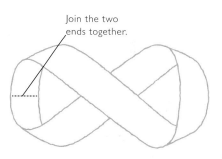

Join the two ends together.

By twisting the completed scarf then joining the two ends, you create a continuous, infinity loop.

HOT DIGGITY DOG BONE

MADE USING A HARDWEARING 100 per cent cotton yarn, this bone stands up to some serious chewing and can be thrown in the wash after a long day of play. Be sure to use machine-washable toy filling, too. The lack of dye in the yarn means that you don't have to worry about having a new pattern on your carpet, or your dog.

YOU WILL NEED

Difficulty
Beginner

Size
22 × 7cm (8½ × 2¾in)

Yarn
One ball of James C Brett Craft Cotton; 100g; 100% cotton. We've used colour Ecru.

Crochet hook
4mm crochet hook

Notions
Polyester toy filling
Blunt-ended yarn needle
Ribbon (optional)

Tension
Tension is not critical on this project, but keep your stitches fairly tight so the toy filling will stay securely inside.

HOW TO MAKE

This is made by creating two branches of the bone and joining them to create one half of the finished bone shape.

First branch
Start with 6dc into magic ring. (6sts)
Rnd 1: 2dc into each st to the end. (12sts)
Rnds 2–4: Dc in each st to end. (12sts)
Cut yarn and fasten off.

Second branch
Make the same as the first branch, but do not break the yarn at the end.

Joining branches
Rnd 1: Dc in the 12sts of circle 2, without breaking yarn dc in the 12sts of circle 1. (24sts)
Rnd 2: (Dc2tog, dc in next six sts) rep to end. (21sts)
Rnd 3: (Dc2tog, dc in next five sts) rep to end. (18sts)
Rnd 4: (Dc2tog, dc in next four sts) rep to end. (15sts)
Rnds 5–14: Dc in each st to the end. (15sts)
Fasten off and stuff firmly with the toy filling.

Making up
Repeat to make a second bone half, the same as the first. Using the blunt-ended yarn needle and a spare scrap of leftover yarn, sew the two halves together to form the full bone. Weave in and cut off any loose ends.

If gifting the bone decorate it by tying a piece of ribbon around the centre, hiding the seam. Make sure to remove the ribbon before giving it to your doggy friend though as it may present a choking hazard. Yikes!

INDUSTRIAL RUBBER CLUTCH

TALK ABOUT A STATEMENT PIECE! This fabulous bag is made from rubber tubing intended for bead crafts. You can use any 6mm (¼in) rubber tubing, just make sure you have the full 25 metre (82 foot) length. Once the rubber is cut it cannot be joined again without looking sloppy, so make sure you do not cut the rubber if you get into a muddle, just unravel it.

YOU WILL NEED

Difficulty
Experienced

Size
Approx 34 x 18cm
(13½ x 7in)

Materials
One package of Beadalon®
6mm (¼in) rubber tubing;
25m (82ft). We've used
colour Jet Black.

Knitting needles
One pair of 12mm
(UKn/a/US17) needles

Notions
Large heat-resistant bowl
or sink
Towel
Large heavy book (optional)
33cm (13in) long zip
40 x 80cm (16 x 32in) lining
fabric
Sewing needle
Matching thread

Tension
There is no set tension or size
for this bag and it may take a
bit of practice to get the hang
of knitting the rubber tubing.

HOW TO MAKE

Tie a loose knot around the two needles, then using the cable cast-on method cast on 26 very loose stitches. The tubing is not that easy to work so make sure the stitches are far too loose for the needles.

Make 7 rows of st st and then cast off so the casting off chain is visible on the knit side of the fabric. Our piece measured about 70cm (27½in) wide and 19cm (7½in) high. Do not cut the end off as you will need this to sew up with.

Your stitches will likely be uneven, so once you have cast off you can work through them individually by pulling the rubber to and fro, evening it out.

Once it's as even as you can manage, use the end of the rubber to sew the two ends of the knit together with an overcast stitch. Then, squash the loop flat and place this seam in the centre of the bag and sew up either side along the bottom.

Make sure your casting-on knot and sewing-up knot are as tight as you can manage. The bag will still look out of shape.

Shaping
Carefully fill a bowl with very hot water and put the knit in, leave it to soften slightly. Then place it on a towel and squash it into shape. We put a towel and a very heavy book on top which set it into shape.

Lining
Once you have your basic knitted outer then you can make a fabric lining. As you will see the lining through the gaps, this needs to be double sided. With right sides together, sew around two pieces of fabric that are the same width but twice the height of your bag. Don't forget to add 1cm (⅜in) around the outside for seam allowance. Leave 3cm (1¼in) of this open and turn the piece right side out. Sew this gap closed. Then, fold one end inside the other and sew a zip along the opening. Tack this onto the rubber all along the top of the lining.

BABY'S DAY OUT HAT

SIMPLE AND QUICK TO KNIT, with no shaping, this cute hat will delight the small person in your life. The pattern is made in one piece, stitched into a hat shape and then gathered at the points to make the ears. Try contrast-colour ribbons at the ears, or even weaving a ribbon in and out of the holes around the turned-up, ribbed edge.

YOU WILL NEED

Difficulty
Beginner

Size
To fit head size:
3–9 months: 45–47cm (17¾–18½in)
9 months–2 years: 48–50cm (19–19¾in)
3–5 years: 50–52cm (19¾–20½in)

Yarn
One ball of Artesano Aran; 100g; 132m (144yds); 50% superfine alpaca and 50% Peruvian Highland wool. We've used colour SFN10 Strathy.

Knitting needles
One pair of 4mm (UK8/US6) needles
One pair of 5mm (UK6/US8) needles

Notions
Blunt-ended yarn needle
70cm (27½in) narrow satin ribbon

Tension
18sts and 24 rows to 10cm (4in) over st st on 5mm (UK6/US8) needles

HOW TO MAKE

Hat
With 4mm (UK8/US6) needles, cast on 83 (87, 91)sts, using the double cast-on method.
Row 1 (RS): K1, *p1, k1; rep from * to end.
Row 2: P1, *k1, p1; rep from * to end.
Rep rows 1 and 2 four (five, six) times more.
Next row: K1, *yfwd, k2tog; rep from * to end.
Next row: As row 2.
Change to 5mm (UK6/US8) needles. Beginning with a knit row, work 40 (42, 44) rows in stocking stitch.
Cast off.

Making up
Fold work in half with right sides together and side edges aligned. Stitch seam on stocking stitch section with backstitch. Turn right sides out and stitch seam on ribbed section with wrong sides together so that the seam will be on the inside when the ribbed band is turned back. Place seam at centre back, then stitch top edges together. Pinch each corner and secure with a few small stitches, then cut ribbon in two equal lengths and tie around each 'ear' in a neat bow.

SUNSHINE HANDBAG

GET YOUR DAILY DOSE OF CHEER with this bright bag. Made in a simple double crochet, the bag will come together quickly. You can make the bag as shallow or deep as you wish, just adjust the number of rounds. Since it is made from t-shirt yarn, the bag with stretch to accommodate all your belongings, then snap back into shape afterwards.

YOU WILL NEED

Difficulty
Beginner

Size
29 x 34cm (11½ x 13½in)

Yarn
One ball of Hoooked Zpagetti; 120m (131yds); 92% cotton, 8% elastane. We've used colour Yellow.

Crochet hook
9mm crochet hook

Notions
Stitch markers
Blunt-ended yarn needle

Tension
8sts and 9 rows to 10cm (4in) over dc on 9mm hook

HOW TO MAKE

With 9mm hook make 26 ch.
Rnd 1: 3dc in 2nd ch from hook, 1dc in each ch to last ch, 3dc in last chain, rotate work 180 degrees and continue to work in bottom of each chain, 23dc, join rnd with sl st to first ch. (52dc)
Place stitch marker in first st of next round and continue in spirals from now on. Do not join rounds. Move the stitch marker up every round.
Rnd 2: 1dc in each dc around, do not join rnd. (52dc).
Rep last row until bag measures 23cm (9in), or the height of your choice.
Handle rnd: 7dc, 11ch, miss next 11dc, 15dc, 11ch, miss next 11dc, dc to end of rnd.
Next round: (1dc in each dc to ch-sp, 11dc in ch-sp) twice, dc to end of rnd. (52dc)
Next rnd: 1dc in each dc around, do not join rnd. (52dc).
Rep last round twice more, joining the round with a sl st to first st on last round.
Fasten off.

Making up
Weave in all ends and block lightly to shape.

TOP TIP

This yarn can vary in thickness due to the manufacturing process, which means your tension may be different to that given. If you find your stitches are loose, try using a smaller hook.

LAZY BONES BASKET

EVERYONE KNOWS THAT CATS LOVE a good place to sit and if it's soft and snug, all the better. This basket is made from stretchy t-shirt yarn that is a by-product from the clothing manufacturing industry. The weight and stretch of each ball varies depending on the material used, but the length is always the same. The basket will fit a small- to medium-sized cat.

YOU WILL NEED

Difficulty
Beginner

Size
38cm (15in) diameter
7.5cm (3in) high

Yarn
One ball of Hoooked Zpagetti; 120m (131yds); 92% cotton, 8% elastane. We've used colour Heart Rose.

Crochet hook
10mm crochet hook

Notions
Stitch marker (SM)
Blunt-ended yarn needle

Tension
8½sts and 10 rows to 10cm (4in) over dc on 10mm hook

HOW TO MAKE

Work 2ch and 6dc into second ch from hook, join round with a sl st to first st.
Rnd 1: 1ch, work 2dc in each st. Do not join. Place SM on last st. (12sts)
Rnd 2: (2dc in next st, 1dc in next st) around. (18sts)
Rnd 3: (2dc in next st, 1dc in next 2sts) around. (24sts)
Rnd 4: (2dc in next st, 1dc in next 3sts) around. (30sts)
Rnd 5: (2dc in next st, 1dc in next 4sts) around. (36sts)
Rnd 6: (2dc in next st, 1dc in next 5sts) around. (42sts)
Rnd 7: (2dc in next st, 1dc in next 6sts) around. (48sts)
Rnd 8: (2dc in next st, 1dc in next 7sts) around. (54sts)
Rnd 9: (2dc in next st, 1dc in next 8sts) around. (60sts)
Rnd 10: (2dc in next st, 1dc in next 9sts) around. (66sts)
Rnd 11: (2dc in next st, 1dc in next 10sts) around. (72sts)
Rnd 12: (2dc in next st, 1dc in next 11sts) around. (78sts)
Rnd 13: (2dc in next st, 1dc in next 12sts) around. (84sts)
Rnd 14: (2dc in next st, 1dc in next 13sts) around. (90sts)
Rnd 15: (2dc in next st, 1dc in next 14sts) around. (96sts)

Rnd 16: (2dc in next st, 1dc in next 15sts) around. (102sts)
Rnd 17: 1dc through back loop in each dc.
Rnd 18 (tweed stitch): 1dc, *1ch, miss next dc, 1dc in next st, rep from * to end.
Rnd 19: 1ch, *1dc into ch sp, 1ch, rep from * to end.
Rep round 19 another four times.
Join with a sl st. Fasten off and weave in ends.

The regular increases create a spiral pattern on the bottom of the basket, not that you'll ever see it through the fur.

URBAN BOBBLE BEANIE

THIS BEANIE SPORTS AN EXTRA-LARGE BOBBLE at the back to weigh down the crown and give it a perfect slouchy look. The ribbing on the bottom band means the hat stays securely in place despite the weight of the bobble, and adjusts to fit nearly any head size. Perfect for throwing on for chilly autumn days or when you're having a bad hair day.

YOU WILL NEED

Difficulty
Moderate

Size
To fit an adult female

Yarn
One ball of Cascade Eco+; 250g; 437m (478yds); 100% wool. We've used colour 0508 Berry.

Knitting needles
One pair of 4.5mm (UK7/US7) needles
One pair of 5.5mm (UK5/US9) needles

Notions
Blunt-ended yarn needle
Cardboard
Sharp scissors

Tension
17sts and 25 rows to 10cm (4in) over blackberry pattern on 5.5mm (UK5/US9) needles

HOW TO MAKE

With 4.5mm (UK7/US7) needles, cast on 102sts using the double cast-on method.
Row 1 (RS): K1, *k1, p1; rep from * to last st, k1.
Rep row 1 another 32 times, ending with a RS row.
Row 34: K2, p1, M1, [(k1, p1) twice, k1, M1, (p1, k1) twice, p1, M1] 9 times, (k1, p1) twice, k1, M1, (p1, k1) twice. (122sts)
Change to 5.5mm (UK5/US9) needles.
Row 35 (RS): Purl.
Row 36: K1, *inc2 in next stitch, p3tog; rep from * to last st, k1.
Row 37: Purl.
Row 38: K1, *p3tog, inc2 in next st; rep from * to last st, k1.
Rows 35–38 set the blackberry pattern. Rep these four rows another eight times.
Row 71: Purl.
Row 72: K1, *p3tog, k1; rep from * to last st, k1. (62sts)
Row 73: Purl.
Row 74: K1, (p3tog) 20 times, k1. (22sts)
Row 75: (P2tog) 11 times. (11sts)
Cut yarn, leaving a long tail, and thread tail through rem 11sts.

Making up
Pull up the tail of yarn at the top, to close up the stitches. Fasten off securely. Fold the hat in half, inside out, and match the two edges. Using the tail, sew the seam on the main part of the hat and the top half of the ribbing using backstitch. Turn right side out and stitch the lower part of the ribbing with wrong sides together, so that the seam will be on the inside when the ribbed band is turned back. Make a pompom and stitch firmly to the crown.

Pompom
Cut two cardboard circles, 12cm (4¾in) in diameter. Cut a 4.5cm (1¾in) hole in the centre of each to create two rings. Hold the two rings together and wind yarn evenly through the centre hole and around the edge until the centre hole is full with the wraps. Using scissors, slip the blade between the two pieces of cardboard and carefully snip through all the loops of the wound yarn. Thread a long length of yarn between the two card rings and around the centre of the pompom, then tie tightly in a firm knot to secure. Remove the cardboard and fluff up the pompom. Trim the pompom with scissors, if necessary, to tidy up the shape.

LIVE WIRE CUFF BRACELET

WORKING WITH WIRE CAN BE HARD ON THE HANDS, so this bracelet uses only the basic double crochet stitch to enhance the beauty of the antique copper colour of the wire – the shade could almost be mistaken for rose gold. Even the basic double crochet stitch can be tough going in wire, so take it slowly and have breaks often to give your hands a rest.

YOU WILL NEED

Difficulty
Beginner

Size
5cm (2in) wide by the length of your choice

Yarn
One ball of Beadsmith Craft Wire, 0.3mm (28 gauge); 36.5m (40yds). We've used colour Antique Copper. Any 0.3mm craft wire will do.

Crochet hook
2mm crochet hook

Notions
Four 5mm (¼in) beads for fastening, or beads of your choice
Blunt-ended needle

Tension
Exact tension is not essential

HOW TO MAKE

With 2mm hook make 14 ch, leaving a long tail before you make the slip knot – enough to sew on four beads.
Row 1: 1 dc in 2nd ch from hook, 1 dc in every following ch to end. (13dc)
Row 2: 1 ch, 1 dc in every st to end. (13dc)
Rep last row until the bracelet is desired length to comfortably fit around your wrist.
Do not fasten off wire.
Button loop row: [4 ch, miss next 2 dc, sl st in next dc] 4 times, 4 button loops made.
Fasten off and weave in end.

Making up
Pull the strip gently into the desired shape, flattening any misshapen stitches on the outer edges.
  Using the long tail at the beginning of the strip, attach four beads evenly along the foundation chain end of the strip, corresponding to the four button loops at the opposite end. Weave in the tail neatly.
  Fasten the bracelet around your wrist – you can manipulate the buttonloops to ensure a secure fasten around the beads.

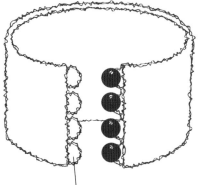

Create button loops to fit over your beads.

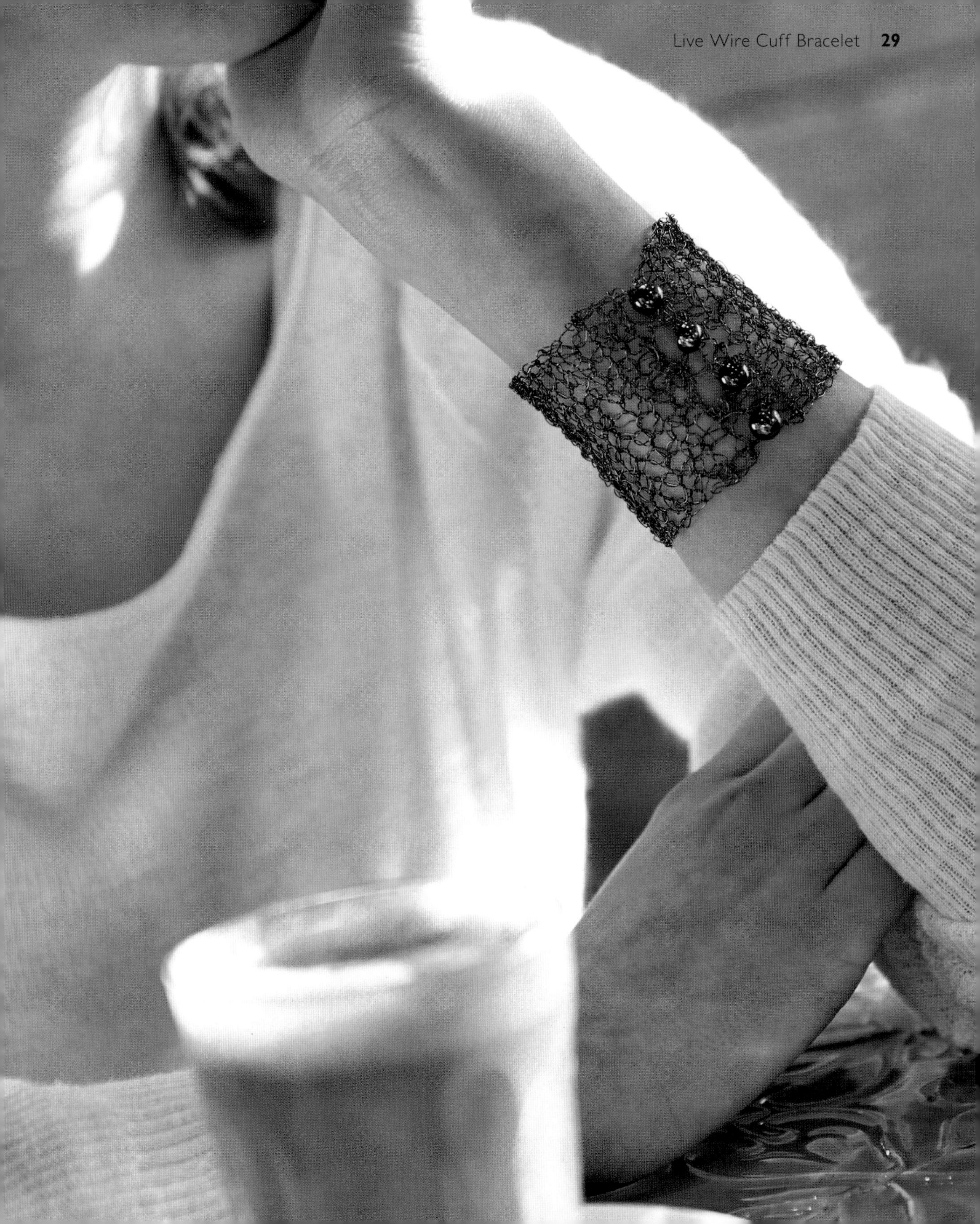

YOU WILL NEED

Difficulty
Experienced

Size
To fit an adult female
60cm (24in) from toe to top

Yarn
One ball of DY Choice Aran
with Wool; 400g; 800m
(875yds); 74% polyacryl, 6%
viscose, 20% wool. We've
used colour 503 Multifleck.

WEEKEND WOOLIES

WHAT'S BETTER THAN WAKING UP on a weekend morning to fresh coffee and comfy slippers? Not much in our opinion. These tall, cabled, slipper-socks are perfect for lounging but they can also do double duty as boot socks. They are knitted flat with a moss stitch sole and no heel, so they're simpler to make than traditional socks and it means one size fits most.

Knitting needles
One pair of 5mm (UK6/US8) needles
Cable needle (CN)

Notions
Blunt-ended yarn needle

Tension
16sts and 25 rows to 10cm (4in) over moss stitch on 5mm (UK6/US8) needles

Special abbreviations
M1 Pick up the horizontal yarn before the next stitch and place it on the left needle to be worked as a new stitch.
M1K indicates to knit this new stitch and **M1P** indicates to purl it
C4B Slip next 2sts onto CN and leave at back, k2, then k2 from CN
C4F Slip next 2sts onto CN and leave at front, k2, then k2 from CN
All cables travel in the same direction per row.

HOW TO MAKE

Both feet
Cast on 58sts using the cable cast-on method.
Row 1: [K2, p2] 14 times, k2.
Row 2: [P2, k2] 14 times, p2.
Rows 3–40: Repeat rows 1 and 2.
Row 41: P6, [k4, p10] 3 times, k4, p6.
Row 42: K6, [p2, M1K, p2, k10] 3 times, p2, M1K, p2, k6. (62sts)
Row 43: P4, p2tog, [k2, p1, M1P, k2, p2tog, p6, p2tog] 3 times, k2, p1, M1P, k2, p2tog, p4. (58sts)
Row 44 and all future even rows unless otherwise specified: follow the stitches in the row below.
Row 45: P3, p2tog, [k2, M1P, p2, M1P, k2, p2tog, p4, p2tog] 3 times, k2, M1P, p2, M1P, k2, p2tog, p3.
Row 47: P2, [p2tog, k2, M1P, p4, M1P, k2, p2tog, p2] 4 times.
Row 49: P1, [p2tog, k2, M1P, p6, M1P, k2, p2tog] 4 times, p1.
Row 51: P2tog, [k2, M1P, p8, M1P, k2, p2tog] 4 times.
Row 53: P1, k2, [p10, C4B for left foot, C4F for right foot] 3 times, p10, k2, p1.
Row 54: K1, [p2, k10, p2, M1K] 3 times, p2, k10, p2, k1. (61sts)
Row 55: P1, [M1P, k2, p2tog, p6, p2tog, k2, p1] 3 times, M1P, k2, p2tog, p6, p2tog, k2, M1P, p1. (58sts)
Row 57: P2, [M1P, k2, p2tog, p4, p2tog, k2, M1P, p2] 4 times.
Row 59: P3, [M1P, k2, p2tog, p2, p2tog, k2, M1P, p4] 3 times, M1P, k2, p2tog, p2, p2tog, k2, M1P, p3.
Row 61: P4, [M1P, k2, p2tog, p2tog, k2, M1P, p6] 3 times, M1P, k2, p2tog, p2tog, k2, M1P, p4.
Row 63: P5, [M1P, k2, p2tog, k2, M1P, p8] 3 times, M1P, k2, p2tog, k2, M1P, p5. (62sts)
Row 64: K6, p2, [p2tog, p1, k10, p2] 3 times, p2tog, p1, k6. (58sts)
Row 65: P6, [C4F for left foot, C4B for right foot, p10] 3 times, C4F for left foot, C4B for right foot, p6. (58sts)
Row 66: K4, [k2tog, p2, M1K, p2, k8] 3 times, k2tog, p2, M1K, p2, k6.
Row 67: P4, [p2tog, k2, p1, M1P, k2, p2tog, p5] 3 times, p2tog, k2, p1, M1P, k2, p2tog, p3. (54sts)
Row 68: K4, [p2, k2, p2, k2tog, k5] 3 times, p2, k2, p2, k2tog, k3. (50sts)
Row 69: P2, [p2tog, k2, M1P, p2, M1P, k2, p2tog, p2] 4 times.
Row 71: P1, [p2tog, k2, M1P, p4, M1P, k2, p2tog] 4 times, p1.
Row 73: [P2tog, k2, M1P, p6, M1P, k2] 4 times, p2tog. (53sts)
Row 74: K1, [p2, k8, p1, p2tog] 3 times, p2, k8, p2, k1. (50sts)
Row 75: P1, k2, [p8, C4B for left foot, C4F for right foot] 3 times, p8, k2, p1.

To be continued... ▶▶▶

Row 76: K1, [p2, k2tog, k6, p2, M1K] 4 times, k1.

Row 77: P2, [k2, p2tog, p3, p2tog, k2, p1, M1P] 3 times, k2, p2tog, p3, p2tog, k2, M1P, p1. (46sts)

Row 78: K2, [p2, k3, k2tog, p2, k2] 4 times. (42sts)

Row 79: [P2, M1P, k2, p2tog, p2tog, k2, M1P] 4 times, p2.

Row 81: [P3, M1P, k2, p2tog, k2, M1P, p1] 4 times, p2. (46sts)

Row 82: [K4, p2, p2tog, p1, k2] 4 times, k2. (42sts)

Row 83: [P4, C4F for left foot, C4B for right foot, p2] 4 times, p2.

Row 84: [K4, p2, M1K, p2, k2] 4 times, k2. (46sts)

Row 85: [P2, p2tog, k2, M1P, p1, k2, p2tog] 4 times, p2. (42sts)

Right foot

Row 87: P1, [k1, p1] 10 times, [p2tog, k2, M1P, p2, M1P, k2, p2tog] 2 times, p1.

Row 88: [K2, p2, k4, p2] 2 times, k1, p21.

Row 89: [K1, p1] 10 times, p2tog, [k2, M1P, p4, M1P, k2, p2tog] 2 times.

Row 90: K1, p2, k6, p1, p2tog, p2, k6, p2, k1, p20.

Row 91: K1, [k1, p1] 10 times, k2, p6, C4F, p6, k2, p1.

Row 92: K1, p2, k6, p2, M1K, p2, k6, p2, k1, p20.

Left foot

Row 87: P1, [p2tog, k2, M1P, p2, M1P, k2, p2tog] 2 times, [p1, k1] 10 times, p1.

Row 88: P21, k1, [p2, k4, p2, k2] 2 times.

Row 89: [P2tog, k2, M1P, p4, M1P, k2] 2 times, p2tog, [p1, k1] 10 times. (43sts)

Row 90: P20, k1, p2, k6, p2, p2tog, p1, k6, p2, k1. (42sts)

Row 91: P1, k2, p6, C4B, p6, k2, [p1, k1] 10 times, k1.

Row 92: P20, k1, p2, k6, p2, M1K, p2, k6, p2, k1. (43sts)

Row 93: P1, M1P, k2, p2tog, p2, p2tog, k2, M1P, p1, k2, p2tog, p2, p2tog, k2, M1P, p1, [p1, k1] 10 times. (42sts)

Row 94: P20, k2, p2, k4, p2, k2,

Row 93: [K1, p1] 10 times, p1, M1P, k2, p2tog, p2, p2tog, k2, p1, M1P, k2, p2tog, p2, p2tog, p2, M1P, p1. (42sts)

Row 94: K2, p2, k4, p2, k2, p2, k4, p2, k2, p20.

Row 95: K2, [p1, k1] 9 times, p2, [M1P, k2, p2tog, p2tog, k2, M1P, p2] 2 times.

Row 96: K3, p2, k2, p2, k4, p2, k2, p2, k3, p20.

Row 97: [K1, p1] 10 times, p3, M1P, k2, p2tog, k2, M1P, p4, M1P, k2, p2tog, k2, M1P, p3. (44sts)

Row 98: K4, p1, p2tog, p2, k6, p1, p2tog, p2, k4, p20. (42sts)

Row 99: K2, [p1, k1] 9 times, p4, C4B, p6, C4B, p4.

Row 100: K4, p2, M1K, p2, k6, p2, M1K, p2, k4, p20. (44sts)

Row 101: [K1, p1] 10 times, p2, p2tog, k2, p1, M1P, k2, p2tog, p2, p2tog, k2, p1, M1P, k2, p2tog, p2. (42sts)

Row 102: K3, p2, k2, p2, k4, p2, k2, p2, k3, p20.

Row 103: K2, [p1, k1] 9 times, p1, [p2tog, k2, M1P, p2, M1P, k2, p2tog] 2 times, p1.

Row 104: K2, [p2, k4, p2, k2] 2 times, p20.

p2, k4, p2, k2.

Row 95: [P2, M1P, k2, p2tog, p2tog, k2, M1P] 2 times, p2, [k1, p1] 9 times, k2.

Row 96: P20, k3, p2, k2, p2, k4, p2, k2, p2, k3.

Row 97: P3, M1P, k2, p2tog, k2, M1P, p4, M1P, k2, p2tog, k2, M1P, p3, [p1, k1] 10 times. (44sts)

Row 98: P20, k4, p2, p2tog, p1, k6, p2, p2tog, p1, k4. (42sts)

Row 99: P4, C4F, p6, C4F, p4, [k1, p1] 9 times, k2.

Row 100: P20, k4, p2, M1K, p2, k6, p2, M1K, p2, k4. (44sts)

Row 101: P2, p2tog, k2, M1P, p1, k2, p2tog, p2, p2tog, k2, M1P, p1, k2, p2tog, p2, [p1, k1] 10 times. (42sts)

Row 102: P20, k3, p2, k2, p2, k4, p2, k2, p2, k3.

Row 103: P1 [p2tog, k2, M1P, p2, M1P, k2, p2tog] 2 times, p1, [k1, p1] 9 times, k2.

Row 104: P20, [k2, p2, k4, p2] 2 times, k2.

Both feet

Rows 105–120: Rep rows 89–104.

Rows 121–128: Rep rows 89–96.

Row 129: K2tog, k18, sl1, k2tog, psso, k17, k2tog. (38sts)

Row 130 and all further even rows: P.

Row 131: K2tog, k16, sl1, k2tog, psso, k15, k2tog. (34sts)

Row 133: K2tog, k14, sl1, k2tog, psso, k13, k2tog. (30sts)

Row 135: K2tog, k12, sl1, k2tog, psso, k11, k2tog. (26sts)

Row 137: K2tog, k10, sl1, k2tog, psso, k9, k2tog. (22sts)

Row 139: K2tog, k8, sl1, k2tog, psso, k7, k2tog. (18sts)

Row 140: Cast off knitwise and pull long end of yarn through.

Making up

Fold each sock right sides together and use a neat overcast stitch to sew across the toe and up the side, matching stitch for stitch.

There is no heel shaping required for these socks, just a different stitch to set the soles apart.

TOP TIP

Pay special attention to the stitch counts throughout to ensure your socks stay on track.

DAPPER DOG

ALWAYS PUT YOUR BEST PAW FORWARD with this doggie bow tie. The yarn we've chosen has metallic flecks in it to make it that little bit extra special. The strap is fastened with press studs, so that the bow tie adjusts to fit a variety of sizes. However, if you need to make the strap longer just continue to follow the pattern for as many extra rows as necessary.

YOU WILL NEED

Difficulty
Beginner

Size
35cm (14in) long strap

Yarn
One ball of James C Brett Twinkle DK; 100g; 300m (328yds); 97% acrylic, 3% polyester. We've used colour 03 Red.

Crochet hook
3.5mm crochet hook

Notions
Blunt-ended yarn needle
Press studs
Matching thread
Sewing needle

Tension
22sts and 25 rows to 10cm (4in) over dc on a 3.5mm hook

HOW TO MAKE

Main bow
Ch 21.
Rnd 1: Dc in 2nd ch from the hook, dc in the next 18sts, 2dc in last ch st, turn and work along the back of the foundation ch, dc in the next 18sts, 2dc in last st. (42sts)
Rnds 2–31: Dc in each st to the end. (42sts)
Fasten off, press flat and sew the opening closed to create a rectangle for the main bow.

Bow middle
Ch 6.
Row 1: Dc in 2nd ch from the hook, dc in the next 4sts. (5sts)
Rows 2–20: Ch 1 turn, dc in each st to end. (5sts)
Fasten off and sew around the main bow, gathering the bow as you go, to form the shape. Weave in and cut off any loose ends.

Strap
Ch 7.
Row 1: Dc in 2nd ch from hook, dc in next 5sts. (6sts)
Rows 1–90: Ch 1 turn, dc in each st to end. (6sts)
Fasten off.

Making up

Sew the middle of the strap to the back of the bow.
Sew press studs to the ends of the bow strap so that it fits on your dog. The strap is slightly stretchy, so if making the bow for a gift add a few press studs, a couple of centimetres apart, so that it will fit a range of dogs.
Weave in and cut off any loose ends.

TEXTING GLOVES

IT'S NO FUN TO FUMBLE WITH YOUR PHONE AND GLOVES on a chilly day, so that's where these come in handy (pun intended). Made with an open thumb and index finger you won't need to remove them to check your phone. That makes life much simpler if it starts to ring or you've lost your way and need to check a map.

YOU WILL NEED

Difficulty
Moderate

Size
To fit an adult female.
Hand circumference
19cm (7½in) and wrist
circumference 16.5cm (6½in)

Yarn
One ball of Juniper Moon
Farm Moonshine; 100g; 180m
(197yds); 40% wool, 40%
alpaca and 20% silk. We've
used colour 14 Popsicle.

Needles
Four 4.5mm (UK7/US7)
double-pointed needles

Notions
Stitch marker
Two stitch holders

Tension
20sts and 30 rows to 10cm
(4in) over st st on 4.5mm
(UK7/US7) needles

HOW TO MAKE

Right glove
Cast on 32sts. Join to work in the round being careful not to twist stitches. Place a stitch marker at the start of the round.
Work 1 round purl.
Work 18 rounds knit.
Inc round 1: K6, M1, k to last 2sts, M1, k2. (34sts)
Work 4 rounds knit.
Inc round 2: K7, M1, k to last 3sts, M1, k3. (36sts)
Work 4 rounds knit.
Inc round 3: K8, M1, k to last 4sts, M1, k4. (38sts)
Work 4 rounds knit.
Thumb set up round: K1, using waste yarn, k6, turn, p6, pick up glove yarn and knit to end of round.
Work 10 rounds knit (or up to base of little finger).

Little finger
K15 sts and put these sts on stitch holder.
K8 sts then put the remaining 15sts on a stitch holder.
Cast-on purlwise 2sts from the last st worked (for the fourchette) and divide these 10sts among three needles. Work 15 rounds knit.
Next round: K2tog to end. (5sts)
Break yarn and thread through remaining sts, draw together and

secure. With a new piece of yarn, pick up 2sts from the fourchette and knit to end of round.

Ring finger
K10 sts and put these sts on stitch holder. K5, pick up 2 fourchette sts, k5 then put the remaining 10sts on a stitch holder. Cast-on purlwise 2sts then divide these 14sts among three needles and work 19 rounds knit.
Next round: K2tog to end. (7sts)
Break yarn and thread through remaining sts, draw together and secure.
With a new piece of yarn, pick up 2sts from the fourchette and knit to end of round.

Middle finger
Put first 5sts and last 5sts on stitch holders for the index finger.
With a new piece of yarn, starting from the front of the glove, k5, pick up 2 fourchette sts, k5, cast-on purlwise 2sts and divide these 14sts among three needles. Work 21 rounds knit.
Next round: K2tog to end. (7sts)
Break yarn and thread through remaining sts, draw together and secure.

Index finger
With a new piece of yarn, pick up 2 fourchette sts, k10, then divide these 12sts among three needles. Work 10 rounds knit.

Work 1 round purl.
Cast off.

Thumb

With a new piece of yarn, pick up
6sts along bottom of waste yarn,
catch ½ of the next st, then 6sts
along the top of the waste yarn and
catch ½ of the next st. (14sts)
Work 1 round knit.
Next round: K5, k2tog, k5, k2tog.
(12sts)
Work 6 rounds knit.
Work 1 round purl.
Cast off.

Left glove

Work as right glove replacing the
following rounds.
Replace increase rounds with the
following:
Inc round 1: K2, M1, k to last 6sts,
M1, k6. (34sts)
Inc round 2: K3, M1, k to last 7sts,
M1, k7. (36sts)
Inc round 3: K4, M1, k to last 8sts,
M1, k8. (38sts)
Replace Thumb set up round with
following:
Thumb set up round: K to last 7sts,
using waste yarn, k6, turn, p6, pick
up glove yarn and k7.

Making up

Weave in any loose ends.

TOP TIP

This hat gives a cabled pattern by twisting the stitches, starting in row 5. The technique used is known as a right twist. It allows you to knit a cable stitch without using a cable needle.

ME & YOU BEANIE

WITH A HINT OF CABLE STITCH MIXED WITH RIBBING, this beanie says both classic and contemporary. It's knitted in a wool-blend of light worsted (DK) weight yarn, so it's soft and comfortable to wear. It comes in one size that will fit most teens and adults. So, you can make one for you, your brother, your sister, your friend and your other half.

YOU WILL NEED

Difficulty
Moderate

Size
The finished hat measures 23cm (9in) across (unstretched) and 31cm (12¼in) long

Yarn
One ball of Sirdar Hayfield DK with Wool; 100g; 300m (328yds); 80% acrylic, 20% wool. We've used colour 97 Fisherfolk.

Knitting needles
One pair of 6.5mm (UK3/US10½) needles

Notions
Blunt-ended yarn needle

Tension
15sts and 18 rows to 10cm (4in) over st st knitted on 6.5mm (UK3/US10½) needles, using yarn doubled

HOW TO MAKE

Using the yarn doubled throughout the pattern, cast on 77 sts.
Row 1: P2, k1tbl, p2, *k4, p2, k1tbl, p2. Rep from * to end.
Row 2: K2, p1tbl, k2, *p4, k2, p1tbl, k2. Rep from * to end.
Row 3: P2, k1tbl, p2, *k4, p2, k1tbl, p2. Rep from * to end.
Row 4: K2, p1tbl, k2, *p4, k2, p1tbl, k2. Rep from * to end.
Row 5: P2, k1tbl, p2, *(k1, k second st on needle, k first st on needle, k1), p2, k1tbl, p2. Rep from * to end.
Row 6: K2, p1tbl, k2, *p4, k2, p1tbl, k2. Rep from * to end.
Rep these six rows six times more.
Row 43: P2, k1tbl, p2, *k4, p2, k1tbl, p2. Rep from * to end.
Row 44: K2, p1tbl, k2, *p4, k2, p1tbl, k2. Rep from * to end.
Row 45: P2, k1tbl, p2, *k4, p2, k1tbl, p2. Rep from * to end.
Row 46: K2, p1tbl, k2, *p4, k2, p1tbl, k2. Rep from * to end.
Row 47: (P1, sl1, k2tog, psso, p1, k1, k second st on needle, k first st on needle, k1) eight times, p1, sl1, k2tog, psso, p1. (59sts)
Row 48: (P2tog) 14 times, p3, (p2tog) 14 times. (31sts)
Row 49: (K2tog) 7 times, k3, (ssk) seven times. (17sts)

Row 50: (P2tog) four times, p1, (p2tog) four times. (9sts)
Break yarn, thread it through rem sts and pull fairly tightly.

Making up
Sew the seam of the hat together using mattress stitch to give a flat seam. Weave in any loose ends.

COLOUR-POP CLUTCH BAG

MADE WITH VISCOSE YARN that has a slight sheen, you can easily take this bag from day to evening. Depending on the yarn and button you choose, this simple pattern can produce any number of different looks, from evening glam to popping to the shops. We've chosen to line our clutch in a bright fabric, but you can have your lining blend in if it's more your style.

YOU WILL NEED

Difficulty
Beginner

Size
29 ×14cm (11½ × 5½in)

Yarn
One ball of Drops Cotton Viscose; 50g; 110m (120yds); 54% cotton, 46% viscose. We've used colour 13 Lavender Blue.

Crochet hook
5mm crochet hook

Notions
Blunt-ended yarn needle
33 x 33cm (13 x 13in)
Matching felt
Fabric glue (optional)
Sewing needle
Matching thread
50cm (20in) lining fabric
Large button
Pins
Tape measure

Tension
17sts and 17 rows to 10cm (4in) over patt on 5mm hook

HOW TO MAKE

Ch 49 sts.
Row 1: Dc in 2nd ch from hook, tr in next ch, (dc in next ch, tr in next ch) repeat to end of chain. (48sts)
Row 2: Ch1, turn, (dc in the next tr, tr in the next dc) rep to end of row. (48sts)
Rep row 2 until your work measures 35cm (13¾in). Weave in any loose ends and fasten off.

Making up
Cut a piece of felt to cover the rectangle, but with the edge sitting just inside the stitches. Sew or use fabric glue to attach the felt to the bag. This stiffens the bag and is hidden by the contrast lining.

Fold the rectangle as follows to form the bag shape:
With the felt side up, fold the bottom edge up 13cm (5in) towards the top. Then, fold the free part of the top edge down. This creates the bag shape. Press lightly to mark the folds, then unfold.

Sew an 8cm (3in) loop of spare yarn to the middle of the top edge of the bag to form the button loop. The ends will be hidden by the lining.

Lining
Cut fabric slightly larger than the flat bag. With wrong side facing, hem the raw edges of the fabric under and overcast stitch in place on the inside of the bag, so that the lining fabric completely covers the felt.

Fold as before and machine or hand sew together the side seams. Sew a big button of your choice to the front of the bag to finish.

PEEK-A-BOO ARMWARMERS

YOU CAN INSTANTLY MAKE DAINTY, LACY ARMWARMERS more cosy by adding a warm fleece lining. The added benefit is that if you make the lining a contrast shade it will show through the crochet for a splash of colour. Try combining greys and neons for an on-trend look, or choose a yarn and fabric in the same colour for a more subdued design.

YOU WILL NEED

Difficulty
Moderate

Size
To fit an adult female

Yarn
One ball of Sirdar Wool Rich Aran; 100g; 190m (208yds); 60% wool, 40% acrylic. We've used colour 311 Shingle.

Crochet hook
4mm crochet hook

Notions
Two pieces of 20 x 20cm (8 x 8in) stretchy fleece fabric
Pins
Sewing needle
Matching thread
Blunt-ended yarn needle

Tension
Each motif excluding joining rounds measures approx 9 x 9cm (3½ x 3½in)

Special abbreviations
Puff (Yrh, insert hook into st, yrh and pull through a loop, drawing it up to the height of a htr) 3 times, 7 loops on hook, yrh and pull through all loops on hook
Picot 3ch, sl st back into first ch made

HOW TO MAKE

Make two complete motifs including joining round and six motifs up to round 4. Eight motifs in total; four for each glove.

With 4mm hook make 2 ch.
Rnd 1: [1 puff, 3 ch] six times into second ch from hook. (6 puffs)
Rnd 2: Sl st to 3 ch-sp, 2 ch (counts as htr) 3 htr in same ch-sp, [4htr in next ch-sp] to end, sl st to top of 2 ch to join rnd. (24htr)
Rnd 3: 4 ch, miss 2 htr, 1 dc in sp between second and third htr, 4 ch, miss 4 htr, 1 dc in sp between next 2 htr, *4 ch, miss 2 htr, 1 dc in sp between next 2 htr, 4 ch, miss 4 htr, 1 dc in sp between next 2 htr; rep from * to end, ending with dc at bottom of first ch. (8ch-sps)
Rnd 4: Sl st to next ch sp, 2 ch (doesn't count as st), *(puff, 2 ch, puff, 2 ch, puff) all into same ch-sp, 1 ch, 5htr in next ch-sp, 1ch; rep from * around, join round with sl st to top of first 2 ch.
Joining rnd: Sl st along to second puff at next corner sp, 2 ch (doesn't count as st), puff in puff, picot, *3 ch, miss puff, 1 dc in next 1ch-sp, 3 ch, miss 2 htr, 1 dc in next htr, 3 ch, miss 2 htr, 1 dc in next 1ch-sp, 3 ch, miss puff, ** 1 puff in next puff, picot; rep from * to end, ending last rep at **, join

rnd with sl st to first 2 ch.
Fasten off.
Block all motifs lightly to shape.

Joining motifs
Take one of the motifs that is finished to the joining round (motif one) and join it to a motif finished to round 4 (motif two), with motif one above motif two as follows:
Attach yarn to any central puff of motif two, 2 ch (doesn't count as st), puff in puff, 3 ch, miss puff, 1 dc in next 1ch-sp, 3 ch, miss 2 htr, 1 dc in next htr, 3 ch, miss 2 htr, 1 dc in next 1ch-sp, 3 ch, miss puff, 1 puff in next puff, 1 ch, sl st into picot at corner

Carry on this way... ▶▶▶

TOP TIP

If you'd like a lighter and lacier armwarmer to wear on warmer days, follow the pattern above but leave out the lining. This will leave the lacework open and make the armwarmers thinner.

of motif one, 1 ch, sl st into puff, 1 ch, 1 dc into corresponding ch-sp of motif one, 1 ch, 1 dc into 1 ch-sp of motif two, 1 ch, 1 dc into corresponding ch-sp of motif one, 1 ch, miss 2 htr on motif two, 1 dc into third htr of motif two, 1 ch, 1 dc into corresponding ch-sp of motif one, 1 ch, 1 dc into next 1 ch-sp of motif two, 1 ch, 1 dc into corresponding ch-sp of motif one, 1 ch, miss next puff of motif two, puff into next puff, 1 ch, sl st into corresponding picot of motif one, 1 ch, sl st into puff, complete rest of round as from * to ** of joining round. Fasten off.

For motif three, join to motif one as you joined two to one, joining to motif one along the right side. For motif four, joining in the same way, join to bottom of motif three and to right side of motif two. Now you should have two squares of four motifs, one for each warmer.

Edging

Rejoin yarn to top of glove.
Row 1: 1 ch and work 39 dc evenly along top edge of glove, turn. (39dc)
Row 2: 2 ch, miss 1 dc, [1 puff in next dc, 1 ch, miss next dc] to last stitch, htr in last st, turn. (19 puffs)

Row 3: 1 ch, 1 dc in each puff and ch along, join round with sl st to first ch. (39dc)
Fasten off. Rejoin yarn to bottom edge and repeat edging. Block armwarmers lightly to shape.

Lining

Place the fabric on the wrong side of the armwarmers with right sides of fabric and armwarmers facing, so that the fleecy lining will be inside the gloves. Fabric should lie just below the dc edge round at the top and bottom. Pin into place. Overcast stitch the fabric into place neatly around the entire edge with small stitches.

Fold the double thickness fabric in half lengthways with the fleece fabric inside and sew up the seam from the top of the glove to 6cm (2½in) down the side. Leave a gap of 6cm (2½in) for the thumb, then sew up the remaining bottom 8cm (3¼in) of the seam.

Thumb

Rnd 1: Reattach yarn to bottom of thumb, 1 ch and work 28 dc evenly around thumb gap, join with sl st to first dc.
Rnd 2: 2ch (counts as htr), 1 htr in each dc around, join rnd with sl st to

top of first ch. (29htr)
Rnd 3: 2ch (counts as htr), (2htrtog) 3 times, 1 htr in each htr to last 6 sts, (2htrtog) 3 times, join rnd with sl st in top of first ch. (23htr)
Rnd 4: 1 ch (doesn't count as st), (dc2tog) 3 times, 1 dc in each htr to last 6 sts, (dc2tog) 3 times, join rnd with sl st in top of first ch. (17dc)
Fasten off.

Making up

Weave in all ends using the blunt-ended yarn needle. Block lightly to shape.

The armwarmers are made from motifs that are then joined together. Above is one complete motif.

If you have scraps of leftover yarn lieing around the house you could make your motifs out of them for multi-coloured armwarmers.

RIBBED FISHERMAN'S COWL

THIS CHUNKY, RIBBED COWL works well for both men and women. Although it is knitted in the round, the first two rows are knitted back and forth to help prevent the work from becoming twisted. The small gap in the lower edge can easily be stitched up when you're weaving in the loose yarn ends.

YOU WILL NEED

Difficulty
Beginner

Size
To fit an adult

Yarn
One ball of Cascade Eco+; 250g; 437m (478yds); 100% wool. We've used colour 9447 Forest Heather.

Needles
60cm (24in) long 5mm (UK6/US8) circular needle

Notions
Blunt-ended yarn needle

Tension
17sts and 23 rows to 10cm (4in) over st st on 5mm (UK6/US8) needles

HOW TO MAKE

Pattern
With a 60cm (24in) long 5mm (UK6/US8) circular knitting needle, cast on 180sts, using the double cast-on method.
Row 1 (RS): *K3, p1; repeat from * to end; turn.
Row 2: *K1, p3; repeat from * to end; turn.
Row 3: *K3, p1; repeat from * to end; do not turn but join in the round and continue from beg of row, repeat stitch pattern of k3, p1 in a continuous spiral until work measures 33cm (13in).
Cast off in rib pattern.

Making up
Thread the yarn tail at the beginning of work into a blunt-ended yarn needle and use it to join the ends of the first two rows. Weave in all yarn tails.

TOO COOL FOR SCHOOL BEANIE

MADE WITH SELF-STRIPING YARN this unisex kid's beanie is super street-cool. Our models Ted and Teagan loved a game of tag, sharing the hat back and forth. The 100 per cent acrylic yarn makes this beanie machine washable, perfect for busy kiddos on the go. It's the simplest of hat patterns made entirely from double crochet worked in rounds.

YOU WILL NEED

Difficulty
Beginner

Size
To fit a child, aged 1–4 years

Yarn
One ball of Sirdar Hayfield Colour Rich Chunky; 200g; 325m (355yds); 100% acrylic. We've used colour 0384 Plum Grey.

Crochet hook
6.5mm crochet hook

Notions
Stitch marker
Blunt-ended yarn needle

Tension
13sts and 16 rows to 10cm (4in) over dc on 6.5mm hook

HOW TO MAKE

Make a magic ring and work 8dc into the ring. (8sts)
Place a stitch marker in the first st of the next round and continue in sprials from now on. Do not join rounds. Move the stitch marker up every round.
Rnd 1: 2dc into each st to the end. (16sts)
Rnd 2: (Dc in the first st, 2dc in the next st) rep to end. (24sts)
Rnd 3: (Dc in the first 2sts, 2dc in the next st) rep to end. (32sts)
Rnd 4: (Dc in the first 7sts, 2dc in the next st) rep to end. (36sts)
Rnd 5: (Dc in the first 8sts, 2dc in the next st) rep to end. (40sts)
Rnd 6: (Dc in the first 9sts, 2dc in the next st) rep to end. (44sts)
Rnd 7: (Dc in the first 10sts, 2dc in the next st) rep to end. (48sts)
Rnd 8: (Dc in the first 11sts, 2dc in the next st) rep to end. (52sts)
Rnds 9–27: Dc in each st to the end. (52sts)

Making up
Fasten off and weave in any loose ends.

TOP TIP

Using a stitch marker is invaluable when working in a spiral as it is very easy to miss where a round starts.

TOP TIP

If you want to try the legwar
on for size as you work, trans
the stitches to a long, spare le
of yarn. Remember to keep t
stitch marker in place. Transfe
them back to the needles to
continue knitting.

LOVELY LEGWARMERS

THIS FABULOUS YARN works up into a complicated looking pattern, without any of the fuss of changing colours. If you want solid-coloured legwarmers simply swap the yarn we've used for a similar one of your choice. These are perfect for cool autumn days or simply lounging around the house. Embrace a touch of the '80s without going overboard.

YOU WILL NEED

Difficulty
Beginner

Size
To fit an adult female.
27cm (10¾in) circumference,
41.5cm (16¼in) tall without
cuff turned back

Yarn
One ball of Cascade Heritage
Print; 100g; 400m (437yds)
75% merino wool and 25%
nylon. We've used colour
09 Clouds.

Knitting needles
Four 3mm (UK11/US3)
double-pointed needles
Four 3.25mm (UK10/US3)
double-pointed needles

Notions
Stitch marker
Blunt-ended yarn needle

Tension
30sts and 43 rows to 10cm
(4in) over st st on 3.25mm
(UK10/US3) needles

HOW TO MAKE

With 3mm (UK11/US3) needles, cast on 80sts, making note of the point in the yarn colour change cycle that you start.
Join in the round, being careful not to twist the stitches. Place a stitch marker to indicate the start of round. The leg warmer is worked from top to bottom.
Work 14cm (5½in) of single ribbing (k1, p1 to end on every round).
Change to 3.25mm (UK10/US3) needles.
Work 23cm (9in) of st st.
Change to 3mm (UK11/US3) needles.
Work 4.5cm (1¾in) of single ribbing. Cast off.
Make two, ensuring that you cast on at the same point in the yarn colour cycle as the first leg warmer so that the stripes will match.

Making up
Weave in any loose ends.

PRETTY IN PINK SLIPPERS

KEEP YOUR FEET TOASTY AND STYLISH in these driving-moc-style slippers. We recommend sewing leather soles to the bottom to help keep them from being slippery on hard floors. The slippers are knitted flat and then sewn with an invisible seam up the sole and back. They're very comfortable with lots of room for your toes to spread out.

YOU WILL NEED

Difficulty
Moderate

Size
To fit an adult woman, shoe sizes UK 5-7 (US 7-9)

Yarn
One ball of Rowan Brushed Fleece; 50g; 105m (115yds); 65% wool, 30% alpaca, 5% polyamide. We've used colour 257 Grotto.

Knitting needles
One pair of 4.5mm (UK7/US7) needles

Notions
Stitch markers
Pre-punched leather sole patches
Heavy sewing thread
Sewing needle
Blunt-ended yarn needle

Tension
18sts and 32 rows to 10cm(4in) over st st on 4.5mm (UK7/US7) needles

Special abbreviations
PM Place stitch marker

HOW TO MAKE

Slipper sole
Cast on 70sts using the double cast-on technique.
Row 1: K35, PM, k35.
Row 2: K1, M1, k to 1st before marker, M1, k2, M1, k to last st, M1, k1. (74sts)
Row 3: K to end
Rep rows 2 and 3, four more times. (90sts)
Next row: K1, M1, k to 1st before marker, M1, k1, M1, k1, M1, k to last st, M1, k1. (95sts)

Slipper upper
Rows 1 and 3: K to end.
Row 2: P to end.
Row 4: P43, PM, p9, PM, p43.
Row 5: K to 7sts before marker, ssk twice, k3tog, k9, sl1, k2tog, psso, k2tog twice, k to end. (87sts)
Row 6: P to end.
Rows 7–12: Rep rows 5 and 6 three more times. (63sts)
Row 13: K36, ssk, turn. (62sts)
Row 14: Sl1, p9, p2tog, turn. (61sts)
Row 15: Sl1, k9, ssk, turn. (60sts)
Row 16: Sl1, p9, p2tog, turn. (59sts)
Rows 17–20: Rep rows 15 and 16 twice more. (55sts)
Row 21: Sl1, k9, ssk, k to end. (Do not turn.)

Row 22: Cast off 21sts, p9, p2tog, cast off rem sts.
With RS facing rejoin yarn and continue working over rem 11 sts.
Row 23: Ssk, k to last 2sts, k2tog. (9sts)
Row 24: P to end.
Rows 25 to 27: Rep rows 23, 24 and 23 once again. (5sts)
Cast off purlwise.
Repeat the pattern to make the second slipper.

Making up
Using a blunt-ended yarn needle sew a seam edge-to-edge along the bottom of the sole and the back of the heel using mattress stitch. Sew the leather sole patches in place on the bottom of the slipper. Repeat for the second slipper.

Sew the patches to the bottom.

A garter stitch sole defines the upper from the sole.

The upper is made in stocking stitch.

WALTER'S JUMPER

NO DOG-ABOUT-TOWN would be caught dead without a stylish jumper. Walter's opted for an everyday neutral grey colour, but we think he would look equally as handsome in a red or green. This pattern uses the full ball of the recommended yarn, so be careful of your tension or you may run out of yarn before you're finished.

YOU WILL NEED

Difficulty
Moderate

Size
To fit dog with approximately a 50cm (20in) chest. 46cm (18in) neck to tail

Yarn
One ball of James C. Brett Aztec Aran; 100g; 190m (207yds); 90% acrylic, 10% alpaca. We've used colour 10 grey.

Knitting needles
40cm (16in) long 4.5mm (UK7/US7) circular needle
40cm (16in) long 5mm (UK6/US8) circular needle
Four 4.5mm (UK7/US7) double-pointed needles
Spare needle

Notions
Blunt-ended yarn needle

Tension
18sts and 24 rows to 10cm (4in) over st st on 5mm (UK6/US8) needles

HOW TO MAKE

The jumper
Using the 4.5mm (UK7/US7) circular needle, cast on 80sts.
Join to work in the round.
3 x 1 rib round: *K3, p1; rep from * to end.
Rep this round eight more times.
1 x 1 rib round: *K1, p1; rep from * to end.
Rep this round eight more times.
Change to the 5mm (UK6/US8) circular needle.
Inc round: *K8, M1; rep from * to end. (90sts)
Work 16cm (6¼in) in st st ending with a WS row.

Leg holes
Next round: K12, cast off 10sts, k45, cast off 10sts, k13.
Next round: K12, turn.
Working over group of 25sts, work 11 rows st st, starting and finishing with a purl row.
Next row: K13.
Leave yarn attached at this point and put these 25sts onto a spare needle.
With RS facing, work 12 rows st st on the other 45sts, ending with a purl row.
(Find the other end of the ball and use that to avoid breaking yarn.)
Return to the original yarn.

Next round: K12, cast on 10sts, k45, cast on 10sts, k13.
Work 20 rounds st st.
Next round: Cast off 17sts, k57, cast off 16sts.
Break yarn and reattach with RS facing.
Work back and forth across remaining 57sts.
Row 1: K to end.
Row 2: P to end.
Row 3: Ssk, k to last 2sts, k2tog. (55sts)
Row 4: P to end.
Rep rows 3 and 4 five more times. (45sts)

Keep going! Nearly there... ▶▶▶

TOP TIP

Make sure you do not cast off too tightly so that the leg holes fit comfortably. You'd hate for all your hard work to result in a grumpy dog.

Next row: Sl1, k2tog tbl, psso, k to last 3sts, k3tog. (41sts)
Next row: P to end.
Rep these two rows two more times, then the first of the two rows again. (29sts)
Cast off purlwise.

Legs

Using the 4.5mm (UK7/US7) circular needle, pick up 40sts around the sides of the leg holes, 10 from each side.
Work 9 rows in a 3 × 1 rib.
Cast off in 3 × 1 rib.
Rep for second leg.

Edging

Work a knitted icord edging around the rear edge of the jumper as follows: With 4.5mm (UK7/US7) double-pointed needles, cast on 2sts.
Working from WS:
Row 1: K1, sl1, pick up a stitch through the edge stitch of the jumper and pass sl st over new st, slide sts to other end of RH needle, pull yarn across back. Rep this row, picking up a stitch from almost every row around the edge of the jumper, judging by the size of the stitch.
At the other end, pass first stitch over second and thread yarn through loop to cast off.

TOP TIP

The cowl gathers at the top with a neat drawstring. Thread the drawstring evenly along the top edge to prevent an uneven gather. You want the closure to look neat and tidy.

DOUBLE-TIME HAT

WE LOVE SOMETHING THAT'S MULTI-PURPOSE and this hat, which doubles as a cowl, is just perfection. It's a simple tube with a drawstring threaded through the top edge. Simply tighten the drawstring and tuck it inside to create a slouchy ribbed beanie, or loosen it and pull it down around your neck for a cosy cowl.

YOU WILL NEED

Difficulty
Beginner

Size
To fit an adult.
30cm (11¾in) high by 50cm (19¾in) circumference

Yarn
One ball of Faircroft Junior; 500g; 1,500m (1,640yds); 100% acrylic. We've used colour 3052 Astor.

Crochet hook
5mm crochet hook

Notions
Blunt-ended yarn needle

Tension
18sts and 9 rows to 10cm (4in) over treble pattern on 5mm hook

HOW TO MAKE

Ch 54sts.
Row 1: Tr in the 3rd ch from the hook, tr in each st along ch. (52sts)
Row 2: Ch 2, turn, working in the back loop of the stitch throughout tr in each st to the end. (52sts)
Rep row 2 until your work measures 50cm (19¾in).
Fasten off leaving a long tail of yarn for sewing up.

Making up
Fold in half so the ribbing stripes run vertically and sew together to form a tube. Weave in and cut off any loose ends.

Drawstring
With matching yarn ch 100 sts. Fasten off.
   Thread the cord through a blunt-ended yarn needle and weave through the stitches along the top edge of the tube so that it can be gathered up into a hat. Knot the ends of the cord together to secure in place.
   This can be worn as a neck cowl or with the cord gathered to make a hat. Turn the hat inside out before wearing it if you don't want the cord to show, or tuck the cord through to the other side.

TOP TIP

When working the double crochet along the edges, ensure you work them evenly along both sides so that the tie lies flat.

ALL TIED UP

THE CASUAL TIE IS HAVING A MOMENT in the spotlight. Although this pattern is simple, it's quite a bit of work with all those small stitches. A fabulous project if you want to keep busy but don't want to do too much thinking. Keep your stitches uniform and block the tie once you're finished to keep it from curling.

YOU WILL NEED

Difficulty
Beginner

Size
140cm (55in) in length and 4.5cm (1¾in) wide

Materials
One ball of DMC Petra Thread size 3; 100g; 280m (306yds); 100% mercerized cotton. We've used colour 5500 green.

Crochet hook
3mm crochet hook

Notions
Blunt-ended yarn needle

Tension
30sts and 29 rows to 10cm (4in) over dc on 3mm hook

HOW TO MAKE

Using a 3mm hook, loosely ch12.
Row 1: 1dc in 2nd ch from hook and 1dc in each ch to end. Turn. (11sts)
Row 2: 1ch, 1dc in each st to end. Turn. (11sts)
Rep row 2 until your work measures 140cm (55in). Do not fasten off.

Making up
Sl st in each st to end of row, 1ch, dc evenly along the long edge, at the corner make 1ch, working along the foundation ch, sl st to end, 1ch, dc evenly along the long edge. Fasten off and sew in ends. Block lightly to shape.

EPIC EARWARMER

KEEP YOUR HEAD TOASTY without hat-hair side effects with this super-wide earwarmer. Two press studs at the back allow you to pop it on and off without having to pull it over your head, too. The cable pattern means it's not for beginners, but with a bit of patience anyone could master this project.

YOU WILL NEED

Difficulty
Moderate

Size
To fit an adult female.
58 × 12cm (22¾ × 4¾in) at widest point

Yarn
One ball of King Cole Gypsy Super Chunky; 100g; 92m (101yds); 80% premium acrylic, 20% wool. We've used colour 1556 Fjord.

Knitting needles
One pair of 9mm (UK00/US13) needles
Cable needle (CN)

Notions
Two large press studs
Sewing needle
Sewing thread

Tension
18sts and 15 rows to 10cm (4in) over cable pattern on 9mm (UK00/US13) needles

Special abbreviations
C4F/C4B (Cable 4 Forward/Cable 4 Back) Slip next 2sts onto a CN and hold at front or back of work, k next 2sts from LH needle, then k sts from CN
C6F/C6B (Cable 6 Forward/Cable 6 Back) Slip next 3sts onto a CN and hold at front or back of work, k next 3sts from LH needle, then k sts from CN
C8F/C8B (Cable 8 Forward/Cable 8 Back) Slip next 4sts onto a CN and hold at front or back of work, k next 4sts from LH needle, then k sts from CN

HOW TO MAKE

Using 9mm (UK00/US13) needles cast on 10sts.
Row 1 (RS): K4, p2, k4.
Row 2: P4, k2, p4.
Row 3: C4B, p2, C4F.

Increase to full width
Row 4: P4, (k1, p1) in next st, (p1, k1) in next st, p4. (12sts)
Row 5: C4B, p1, k2, p1, C4F.
Row 6: P4, (k1, p1) in next st, p2, (p1, k1) in next st, p4. (14sts)
Row 7: C4B, p1, k4, p1, C4F.
Row 8: P4, (k1, p1) in next st, p4, (p1,

k1) in next st, p4. (16sts)
Row 9: C4B, p1, C6F, p1, C4F.
Row 10: P4, (k1, p1) in next st, p6, (p1, k1) in next st, p4. (18sts)
Row 11: C4B, p1, k8, p1, C4F.
Row 12: P4, (k1, p1) in next st, p8, (p1, k1) in next st, p4. (20sts)
Row 13: C4B, p1, k10, p1, C4F.
Row 14: P4, (k1, p1) in next st, p10, (p1, k1) in next st, p4. (22sts)

Cable pattern repeat
Row 15: C4B, p1, C8B, k4, p1, C4F.
Rows 16, 18 and 20: P4, k1, p12, k1, p4.
Rows 17 and 19: C4B, p1, k12, p1, C4F.
Row 21: C4B, p1, k4, C8F, p1, C4F.
Rows 22, 24 and 26: As row 16.
Rows 23 and 25: As row 17.
These last 12 rows (15 to 26) form the cable patt rep.
Rep these 12 rows four times more (or to length required).

Decrease end
Next row: C4B, p2tog, C6B, k4, p2tog, C4F. (20sts)
Next row: P4, k1, p10, k1, p4.
Next row: C4B, p2tog, K8, p2tog, C4F. (18sts)
Next row: P4, k1, p8, k1, p4.
Next row: C4B, p2tog, K6, p2tog, C4F. (16sts)
Next row: P4, k1, p6, k1, p4.
Next row: C4B, (p2tog, C4F) twice. (14sts)

Next row: P4, (k1, p4) twice.
Next row: C4B, p2tog, k2, p2tog,
C4F. (12sts)
Next row: P4, k1, p2, k1, p4.
Next row: C4B, (p2tog) twice,
C4F. (10sts)
Next row: P4, k2, p4.
Next row: C4B, p2, C4F.
Next row: P4, k2, p4.
Cast off evenly in rib as set.

Making up

Sew in all ends. Overlap the cast-on
end over the cast-off end by approx
6cm (2½in) (or to fit) and mark
position of the two press studs.
Sew press studs to each end
where marked.

Overlap the two ends at the
back and close them with press
studs. Adjust the position of the
press studs so that you have a
good fit around your head.

SEA MONSTER TEASER

THIS 16-LEGGED SEA MONSTER is sure to catch your cat's eye. No cat can resist a squiggly, wriggly thing in motion. The tentacles are made in a strip that is coiled up and then inserted into the bottom of the body. To entice even the laziest of cats you can try adding some dried cat nip to the toy filling, or tie the hanging cord to the end of a pole.

YOU WILL NEED

Difficulty
Moderate

Size
Approx 22cm (8¾in) tall, excluding cord

Yarn
One ball of Adriafil New Zealand Print; 100g; 200m (219yds); 75% wool, 25% acrylic. We've used colour 046 Bright Multicolour.

Knitting needles
One pair of 4.5mm (UK7/US7) double-pointed needles

Notions
Polyester toy filling
Scraps of black and white or yellow felt
Sewing needle
Embroidery or sewing thread to match your felts
Blunt-ended yarn needle

Tension
20sts and 25 rows to 10cm (4in) over st st on 4.5mm (UK7/US7) needles

HOW TO MAKE

Tentacles
*Using two 4.5mm (UK7/ US7) double-pointed needles, cast on 4sts.
Row 1: K4; do not turn but slide sts to other end of needle.
Rep row 1 39 more times. Cut yarn and transfer to a spare needle.**
Rep from * to ** 15 times more; do not cut yarn after making 16th tentacle.

Core
Row 1: Cast on 50sts, k these sts, k4 sts from last tentacle, then k across all sts on spare needle, turn. (114sts)
K 5 rows. Cast off.

Body
Using two 4.5mm (UK7/US7) double-pointed needles, cast on 36sts using the cable cast-on method.
Beg with a k row, work 12 rows st st.
Row 13: (K4, k2tog) 6 times. (30sts)
Row 14: Purl.
Row 15: (K3, k2tog) 6 times. (24sts)
Row 16: Purl.
Row 17: (K2, k2tog) 6 times. (18sts)
Row 18: Purl.
Row 19: (K1, k2tog) 6 times. (12sts)
Row 20: (P2tog) 6 times.
Cut the yarn and use the blunt-ended yarn needle to thread the tail through rem 6sts.

Hanging cord
Using two 4.5mm (UK7/US7) double-pointed needles, cast on 2sts.
Row 1: K2; do not turn but slide sts to other end of needle.
Rep row 1 59 more times.
Cast off.

Making up
Starting at the end without the tentacles, roll up the core strip into a fairly tight coil, securing it with a few stitches as you go. When you reach the tentacles, continue rolling, using the tail of yarn at the top of each tentacle to secure it to the core and weaving the remaining end into the layers of knitting.

Stitch the side seam on the body. Place the body over the core and stitch the cast-on edge to the top of the tentacles all around.

Insert some toy filling through the small hole at the top of the body, then insert one end of the hanging cord; pull up the yarn tail to close up the hole and trap the end of the hanging cord, then secure with a few small stitches.

Cut circles of felt for the eyes and stitch in place on the body using sewing or embroidery thread.

GRANNY-CHIC COIN PURSE

KEEP ALL YOUR LOOSE CHANGE and any other stray items in your handbag safe and secure in this little purse. It's fully lined so even the smallest items won't slip out. It's made from two round motifs that are sewn along the bottom and then attached to a pre-made clasp frame at the top. It's so retro-cool both your friends and your grandmother will be envious.

YOU WILL NEED

Difficulty
Moderate

Size
10 x 11.5cm (4 x 4½in)

Yarn
One ball of Phildar Phil Coton 4; 50g; 85m (93yds); 100% cotton. We've used colour 040 Outremer.

Crochet hook
4mm crochet hook

Notions
15 x 25.5cm (6 x 10in) lining fabric
9cm (3½in) wide purse frame
Sewing needle
Matching thread
Blunt-ended yarn needle

Tension
The first round measures approx 3.5cm (1⅜in) diameter

Special abbreviations
Bobble stitch Yrh, insert hook in stitch, yrh, draw loop through, yrh, draw through 2 loops on the hook, (yrh, insert hook in same space, yrh, draw loop through, yrh, draw through 2 loops on hook) rep 3 times, yrh, draw through all 6 loops on hook

HOW TO MAKE

Purse rounds
Make two.
Ch 4, sl st in first ch to form ring.
Rnd 1: Ch 3 (bobble st, ch 2 into ring), rep 5 more times, join with sl st to first bobble. (6 bobbles, 6ch spaces)
Rnd 2: Ch 3, (bobble st, ch2, bobble st, ch2) in each ch space to end, join with sl st to first bobble. (12 bobbles, 12 ch spaces)
Rnd 3: Ch 3, (bobble st, ch2, bobble st, ch2 in next ch space, bobble st, ch2 in next ch space), rep to end, join with sl st in first bobble. (18 bobbles, 18 ch spaces)
Rnd 4: Ch3, 2tr in same ch space, 3tr in next 6 ch spaces, 3dc in the remaining ch spaces. (54sts)
Rnd 5: Dc in each st to the end. (54sts)
Fasten off leaving a long tail of yarn to sew together.
Making sure the treble stitches from round 4 are at the top, sew together leaving a 10cm (4in) gap at the top of the purse.

Lining
Cut two circles of lining fabric a few cms (1in) larger than the purse rounds. Sew together leaving a third open at the top. Place inside the purse, turn the hem at the top to the back and sew in place.

Using matching thread, sew the purse to the purse frame using the holes along the frame edge.
Weave in any loose ends and fasten off well.

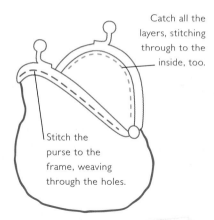

Catch all the layers, stitching through to the inside, too.

Stitch the purse to the frame, weaving through the holes.

TOP TIP

Be sure to use very small
stitches when sewing the
lining in place, or your
fingers and rings may catch
on the thread when you
reach in.

MARLED SCARF

THIS SCARF IS JUST THE RIGHT LENGTH to tie around your neck for a bit of extra warmth and style. The merino wool yarn we've used is super soft. If you'd prefer a longer scarf you can follow the pattern using a longer ball of yarn, or you can join two balls of yarn. Shhhh, we won't tell anyone that it's not just one ball if you don't!

YOU WILL NEED

Difficulty
Moderate

Size
16 x 78cm (6¼ x 30¾in)

Yarn
One ball of Malabrigo Mecha; 100g; 120m (131yds); 100% merino wool. We've used colour 043 Plomo.

Knitting needles
One pair of 8mm (UK0/ US11) needles

Notions
Contrasting DK weight yarn for tassels (optional)
Crochet hook for tassels and casting on

Tension
16sts and 18 rows to 10cm (4in) over pattern on 8mm (UK0/US11) needles

HOW TO MAKE

Scarf
Cast on 26sts using the crochet cast-on method.
Row 1: K3, *yfwd, skpo, k2; rep from * to last 3sts, yfwd, skpo, k1.
Row 2: P3, *yfwd, p2tog, p2; rep from * to last 3sts, yfwd, p2tog, p1.
Rep rows 1 and 2 until a small amount of yarn remains.
Cast off.
For a longer, skinny scarf, cast on 18sts and work in the same way.

Tassels
If you'd like, add tassels to the scarf using scraps of DK weight yarn. Wind yarn around four of your fingers and cut to make 36 strands, each approx. 38cm (15in) long. Make six tassels across both ends of the scarf by folding the strands in half in groups of three and inserting a crochet hook up through a stitch along the edge; draw the strand through to the back. Pass the ends of the strand through the loop and tighten.

TOP TIP

Make sure you keep the same tension across each row, particularly on the first and last stitch, so that the scarf lies flat.

TECHNIQUES

TOOLS OF THE TRADE

THERE IS NO END TO THE SUPPLIES that are available for knitting and crochet, so you're sure to be able to find some to match your taste and budget; from the most basic needles and hooks to the more bespoke. Below is a selection of the most common tools you will need to complete the projects in this book. Always read through the tools and materials section for each pattern first to see if there is anything extra you might need.

PRESS STUDS

Useful for projects needing a fastening, without having to work a button hole.

ROW COUNTER

Sit this on the end of your needle and change the number when you complete a row.

WOOL

The choices are almost endless. Choose one with the correct weight for your pattern.

SCISSORS

Keep a pair of good-quality, sharp scissors to hand for cutting yarn and trimming ends.

STITCH MARKERS

CIRCULAR NEEDLE

A flexible tube joins two needles for circular knitting. These needles come in different lengths.

CROCHET HOOKS

Hooks are available in different materials and sizes. Choose one that is comfortable.

STITCH HOLDERS

Slide your work onto a stitch holder when you're not working it to keep it neat.

TAPE MEASURE

KNITTING NEEDLES

Available in different materials and sizes, choose the one that is right for each project.

BLUNT-ENDED NEEDLE

The blunt tip prevents damage to the yarn when darning in ends or sewing up.

SEWING NEEDLE

PINS

DOUBLE-POINTED NEEDLES

CABLE NEEDLES

KNITTING

THE TECHNIQUES THAT FOLLOW will help you complete the knitting patterns in this book, if you need to quickly brush up on anything you may have forgotten. Don't worry, it happens to the best of us.

CASTING ON

SINGLE CAST-ON (thumb cast-on)

1 Hold the needle with the slip knot in the right hand. Then, wrap the yarn around the left thumb as shown and hold the yarn in place in the palm of the left hand.

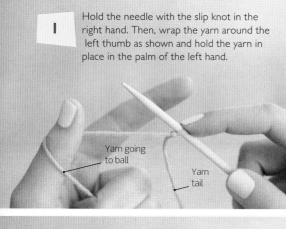

Yarn going to ball

Yarn tail

2 Insert the needle tip under and up through the loop on the thumb. Release the loop from the thumb and pull the yarn to tighten the new cast-on loop on the needle, sliding it up close to the slip knot.

3 Loop the yarn around the thumb again and continue making loops in the same way until the required number of stitches is cast on to the needle.

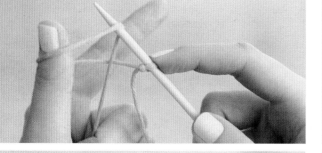

Yarn going to ball

Yarn tail

CABLE CAST-ON

1 Hold the needle with the slip knot in the right hand. Then knit-stitch cast-on one stitch onto the left needle. Insert the tip of the right needle between the two stitches. Wrap the yarn under and around the tip of the right needle.

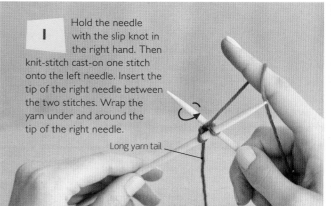

Long yarn tail

2 With the tip of the right needle, draw the yarn under and through to the front to form a loop on the right needle.

3 Transfer the loop to the left needle by inserting the tip of the left needle from right to left through the front of the loop. Continue, inserting the right needle between the first two loops on the left needle for each new cast-on stitch.

DOUBLE CAST-ON (long-tail cast-on)

1 Make a slip knot on the needle, leaving a very long yarn tail – about 3.5cm (1⅜in) for each stitch to be cast on. Hold the needle in your right hand. Then wrap the yarn around the left thumb as shown and hold the yarn in place in the palm of the left hand.

Yarn going to ball

Long yarn tail

2 Insert the tip of the needle under and up through the loop on the thumb.

3 Wrap the long yarn tail around the needle counter-clockwise.

4 Release the loop from the thumb, over the tip of the needle.

5 Pull both yarn ends to tighten the new cast-on loop on the needle, sliding it up close to the slip knot.

6 Loop the yarn around the thumb again and cast on another stitch in the same way. Make as many stitches as you need.

Yarn going to ball

Yarn tail

CROCHET CAST-ON

1 Make a slip knot on a crochet hook. Hold yarn and knitting needle in the left hand and hook in the right. Take the yarn behind the needle and over left index finger. Hold needle and hook crossed, with the hook in front.

2 Catch the yarn in the hook using left index finger. Pull the yarn through the slip knot. The yarn will loop over the needle making a stitch. Take the yarn behind the needle and make another loop in the same way. Continue to cast on the required number of stitches.

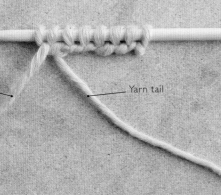

CASTING OFF

CASTING OFF KNITWISE

1 Begin by knitting the first two stitches. Then insert the tip of the left needle from left to right through the first stitch and lift this stitch up and over the second stitch.

2 Slide the stitch off the right needle. To cast off the next stitch, knit one more stitch and repeat Step 1. (If your pattern says "cast off in pattern", work the stitches in the specified pattern [knitwise or purlwise] as you cast off.)

3 Continue until only one stitch remains on the right needle. To stop the last stitch from unravelling, cut the yarn, leaving a yarn tail long enough to darn in later. Pass the yarn end through the final loop and pull tight. This is called "fastening off".

CASTING OFF PURLWISE

1 Purl two stitches. Insert the tip of the left needle into the first stitch and pass it over the second stitch and off the right needle.

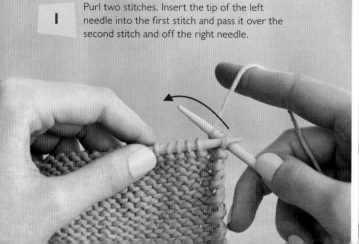

2 Repeat across the row, but purl only one stitch in Step 1 for all remaining stitches. Fasten off the last stitch.

KNIT & PURL STITCHES

All knitting is made up of only two basic stitches – knit and purl. These examples below are shown on stocking stitch. The purl stitch can be a little more difficult, but becomes effortless with practice.

KNIT STITCH (abbreviation: k)

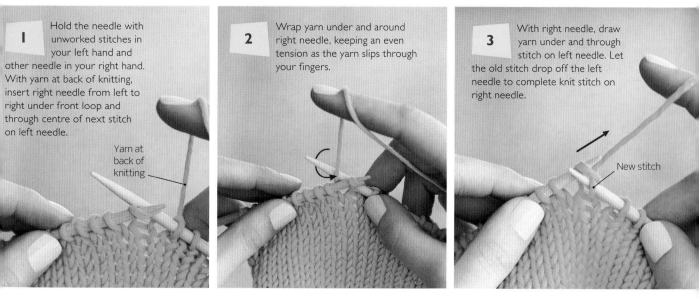

1 Hold the needle with unworked stitches in your left hand and other needle in your right hand. With yarn at back of knitting, insert right needle from left to right under front loop and through centre of next stitch on left needle.

Yarn at back of knitting

2 Wrap yarn under and around right needle, keeping an even tension as the yarn slips through your fingers.

3 With right needle, draw yarn under and through stitch on left needle. Let the old stitch drop off the left needle to complete knit stitch on right needle.

New stitch

PURL STITCH (abbreviation: p)

1 With yarn at front of knitting, insert right needle from right to left through centre of next stitch to be worked on left needle.

Yarn at front of knitting

2 Wrap yarn over and around right needle. Keep an even tension on the yarn as you release it.

3 With right needle, draw yarn back and through stitch on left needle. Keep your hands relaxed. Let the old stitch drop off the left needle to complete purl stitch.

Completed new stitch

Old stitch

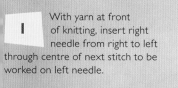

CONTINENTAL KNITTING

In Continental-style knitting the yarn is held in the left hand as you work instead of the right hand. Because of this, the basic knit and purl stitches are worked slightly differently. If you knit in this way, follow the steps below for reference. If you don't normally knit this way, why not try something new?!

HOLDING THE YARN "CONTINENTAL" STYLE

1 Lace the yarn through the fingers of the left hand in any way that feels comfortable. Try to both release and tension the yarn easily to create uniform loops.

2 Hold the needle with the unworked stitches in the left hand and the other needle in the right hand. Position the yarn with the left forefinger and pull it through the loops with the tip of the right needle.

In this alternative version the yarn is wrapped twice around the forefinger and then over the other fingers.

For both the knit and purl stitches wrap the yarn around your left little finger, but keep it over all your other fingers, this makes purling easier.

CONTINENTAL KNIT STITCH

1 Hold your index finger up with the yarn over it and use your middle finger to hold the yarn against the left needle, slightly forwards of the stitch.

2 Insert the right needle up into the front of the stitch. Take it up, over and behind the yarn and pull it through the stitch to the front.

3 Slide the old stitch off the left needle. At the end of the row, keep the yarn around your left fingers. Swap the needles to start the next row.

CONTINENTAL PURL STITCH

1 Bring the yarn to front. With your index finger raised and your middle finger touching the left needle near the tip, insert the needle into the first stitch as for purl.

2 Tilt the right tip towards you and then back in a small circular movement so that the yarn wraps over it. Keep your index finger in constant contact with the left needle.

3 At the same time, bring your left index finger with the yarn on it forwards, wrapping the yarn around the needle. Immediately dip the right needle tip away from you to hook the yarn.

4 Take the needle backwards through the old stitch and make a new purl loop. Slide the old stitch off the left needle.

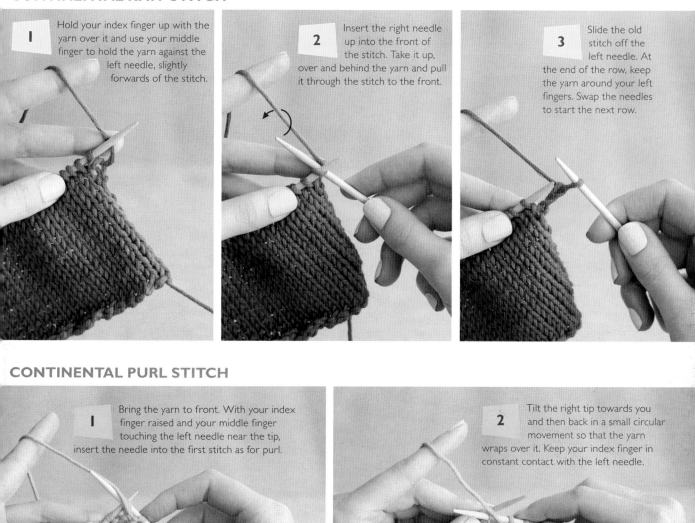

GARTER STITCH (abbreviation: g st)

Forms horizontal ridges

Edges of fabric lie flat and do not roll

Knit all rows: Garter stitch is the easiest of all flat knitted fabrics because whichever side is facing you, all rows are worked in knit stitch. Both sides look the same. The resulting fabric is soft, textured, and slightly stretchy. More rows are needed than in stocking stitch (below) to make the same length of fabric.

SINGLE RIBBING (abbreviation: k1, p1 rib)

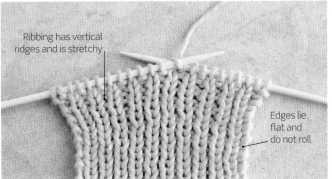

Ribbing has vertical ridges and is stretchy

Edges lie flat and do not roll

Work alternate knit and purl stitches: Single ribbing is formed by working alternating knit and purl stitches across a row. After a knit stitch, take the yarn to the front between the needles to purl the next stitch. After a purl stitch, take the yarn to the back between the needles to knit the next stitch. On the wrong-side rows, knit all the knit stitches and purl all the purl stitches.

STOCKING STITCH (abbreviation: st st)

1 Stocking stitch is formed by working alternate rows of knit and purl stitches. When the right side is facing you, knit all the stitches in the row.

Side edges roll slightly to back

Right side is smooth

2 When the wrong side is facing you, purl all the stitches in the row.

Wrong side is bumpy

KNITTING THROUGH BACK OF LOOP
(abbreviation: k1 tbl or kb)

1 Insert the right needle from right to left, through the side of the stitch, behind the left needle (called the back of the loop).

2 Wrap the yarn around the tip of the right needle and complete the knit stitch in the usual way. This twists the stitch in the row below so that the legs of the stitch cross at the base.

SLIPPING STITCHES PURLWISE
(abbreviation: s, sl1 or sl1p)

1 Always slip stitches purlwise, unless instructed otherwise. Insert the tip of the right needle from right to left through the front of the stitch on the left needle.

2 Slide the stitch onto the tip of the right needle and off the left needle without working it.

SLIPPING STITCHES KNITWISE
(abbreviation: s, sl1 or sl1k)

1 Slip stitches knitwise only if instructed to do so, or if working decreases, as it twists the stitch. Insert the tip of the right needle from left to right through the front of the loop on the left needle.

2 Slide the stitch onto the right needle and off the left needle without working it. The slipped stitch now sits on the right needle with the left side of the loop at the front.

INCREASES

"MAKE ONE" LEFT CROSS INCREASE ON A KNIT ROW (abbreviation: M1 or M1K)

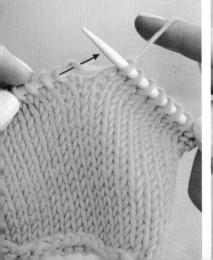

1 Insert the tip of the left needle from front to back under the horizontal strand between the stitch just knit and the next stitch.

2 Then insert the right needle through the strand on the left needle from right to left and behind the left needle.

3 Wrap the yarn around the tip of the right needle and draw the yarn through the lifted loop. This creates an extra stitch in the row.

"MAKE ONE" INCREASE ON PURL ROW (abbreviation: M1 or M1P)

1 Insert the tip of the left needle from front to back under the horizontal strand between the stitch just knit and the next stitch.

2 Then insert the right needle through the strand on the left needle from left to right from behind the left needle to the front.

3 Wrap the yarn around the tip of the right needle and draw the yarn back through the lifted loop (known as purling through the back of the loop.) This creates an extra stitch.

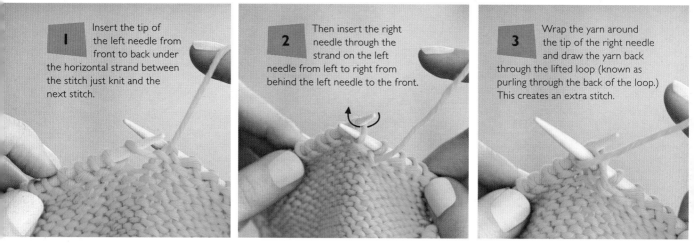

MULTIPLE INCREASES (abbreviation: Inc2 or [k1, p1, k1] into next st)

This is a very easy increase if you need to add more than one stitch to an existing stitch, but it does create a small hole under the new stitches.

1 To begin the increase, knit the next stitch but leave the old stitch on the left needle.

Old stitch

2 Then purl and knit into the same stitch on the left needle. This action is called knit one, purl one, knit one all into the next stitch. It creates two extra stitches in the row. You can keep alternating knit and purl stitches in the same loop to create even more stitches if needed.

K1
P1
K1

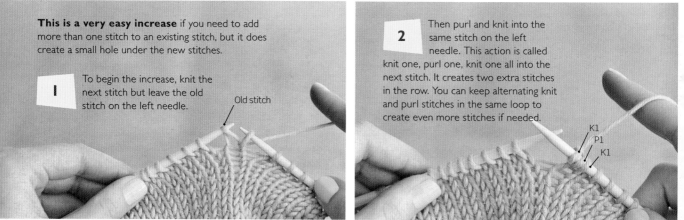

YARNOVER BETWEEN KNIT STITCHES (abbreviation: UK yfwd; US yo)

1 Bring the yarn to the front of the knitting between the needles. Take the yarn over the top of the right needle to the back and work the next knit stitch in the usual way.

2 When the knit stitch is complete, the yarnover is correctly formed on the right needle with the right leg of the loop at the front.

3 On the following row, when you reach the yarnover, purl it through the front of the loop in the usual way. This creates an open hole under the purl stitch.

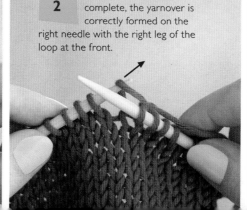

YARNOVER BETWEEN PURL STITCHES (abbreviation: UK yfrn and yon; US yo)

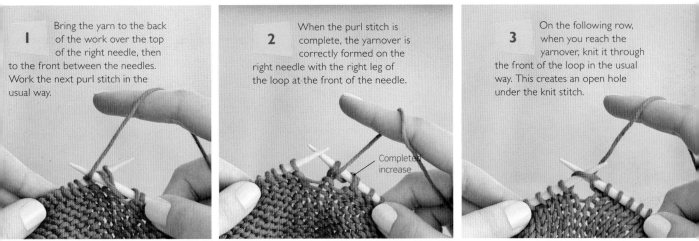

1 Bring the yarn to the back of the work over the top of the right needle, then to the front between the needles. Work the next purl stitch in the usual way.

2 When the purl stitch is complete, the yarnover is correctly formed on the right needle with the right leg of the loop at the front of the needle.

Completed increase

3 On the following row, when you reach the yarnover, knit it through the front of the loop in the usual way. This creates an open hole under the knit stitch.

DECREASES

KNIT TWO TOGETHER (abbreviation: k2tog or dec 1)

1 Insert the tip of the right needle from left to right through the second stitch then the first stitch to be worked on the left needle.

2 Wrap yarn under and around right needle, draw the yarn through both loops and drop the old stitches off the left needle.

3 This makes two stitches into one and decreases one stitch in the row. The completed stitch slants to the right.

PURL TWO TOGETHER (abbreviation: p2tog or dec 1)

1 Insert the tip of the right needle from right to left through the first then the second stitch on the left needle.

2 Wrap the yarn around the tip of the right needle, draw the yarn back through both loops and drop the old stitches off the left needle.

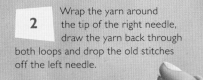

3 This makes two stitches into one and decreases one stitch in the row.

SLIP, SLIP, KNIT (abbreviation: ssk)

1 Slip the next two stitches on the left needle knitwise, one at a time, onto the right needle without working them.

Slipped stitches

2 Insert the tip of the left needle from left to right through the fronts of the two slipped stitches (the right needle is now behind the left).

3 Knit these two stitches together. This makes two stitches into one and decreases one stitch in the row.

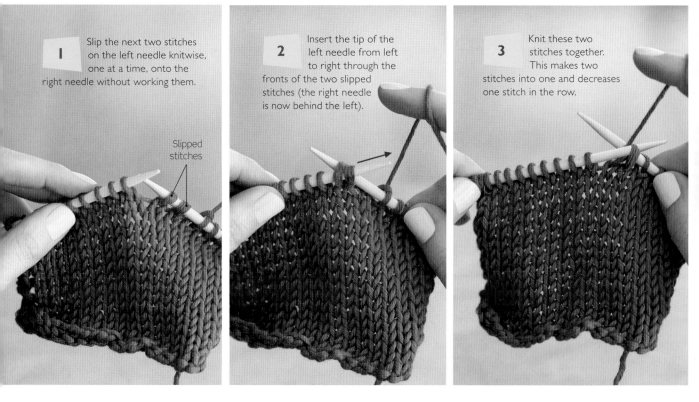

SLIP ONE, KNIT ONE, PASS SLIPPED STITCH OVER (abbreviation: sl kl psso or skpo)

1 Slip the first stitch on the left needle knitwise onto the right needle without working it. Knit the next stitch.

Slipped knitwise onto right needle

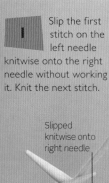

2 Pick up the slipped stitch with the tip of the left needle and pass it over the knit stitch and off the right needle.

3 This makes two stitches into one and decreases one stitch in the row.

KNIT THREE TOGETHER (abbreviation: k3tog)

1 Insert the tip of the right needle from left to right through the third stitch on the left needle, then the second, then the first. Knit these three together. This decreases two stitches at once.

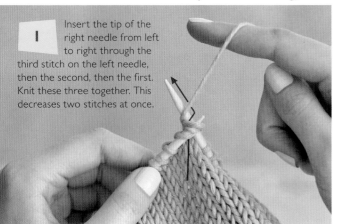

PURL THREE TOGETHER (abbreviation: p3tog)

2 Insert the tip of the right needle from right to left through the first, second, and third stitch on the left needle. Purl these three together.

WORKING WITH A CIRCULAR NEEDLE

1 Cast on the required number of stitches. Ensure that the stitches are untwisted and they all face inwards, then slip a stitch marker onto the end of the right needle to mark the beginning of the round.

Stitch marker

If you are working a stocking stitch tube on a circular needle, the right side of the work will always be facing you and every round will be a knit round.

2 Hold the needle ends in your hands and bring the right needle up to the left needle to work the first stitch. Knit round and round on the stitches. When the stitch marker is reached, slip it from the left needle to the right needle.

Stitches all face inwards

CABLES

Cables are usually worked in stocking stitch on a reverse stocking stitch (or garter stitch) ground. They are made by crossing two, three, four or more stitches over other stitches in the row. This technique is illustrated here with the cable 4 front and cable 4 back cables. The principle is the same no matter how many stitches you are cabling.

CABLE 4 FRONT (abbreviation: C4F)

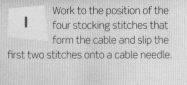

1 Work to the position of the four stocking stitches that form the cable and slip the first two stitches onto a cable needle.

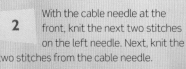

2 With the cable needle at the front, knit the next two stitches on the left needle. Next, knit the two stitches from the cable needle.

3 This creates a cable crossing that slants to the left. For this reason, a "front cable" is also called a "left cable".

CABLE 4 BACK (abbreviation: C4B)

1 Work as for Step 1 of Cable 4 front, but place the cable needle at the back of the knitting.

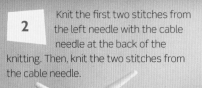

2 Knit the first two stitches from the left needle with the cable needle at the back of the knitting. Then, knit the two stitches from the cable needle.

3 This creates a cable crossing that slants to the right. For this reason, a "back cable" is also called a "right cable".

CROCHET

THE TECHNIQUES THAT FOLLOW will act as a handy reference to help you complete the crochet patterns. There are only a few basic stitches that you need to master. Remember, practice makes perfect!

FOUNDATION CHAIN (abbreviation: ch)

1 Start with a slip knot on your hook. Wrap the yarn around the hook; this action is called "yarn round hook" (abbreviated yrh). Move your hook under the yarn at the same time as you move the yarn slightly forwards and down.

Wrap the yarn over and around the hook

2 With the yarn gripped in the lip of the hook, draw a loop of yarn through the loop on the hook. (Hold the base of the slip knot with the free fingers of your yarn hand as you draw the loop through.)

Pull yarn loop through in the direction of the arrow

3 Continue Steps 1 and 2 until you have the required number of chains.

Front of foundation chain

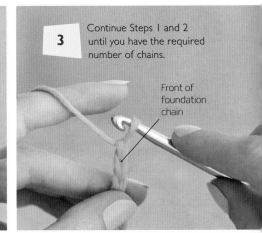

COUNTING CHAIN STITCHES

Counting correctly: As you make chains for the foundation chain, count each stitch until you have made the required number. Then, before starting your crochet, recount the chains to check that you have the correct number. With the front of the chain facing you, start counting the stitches from the base of your hook leftwards.

Do not count loop on hook

SLIP STITCHES (abbreviation: sl)

1 Start by working a foundation chain in the desired length. To make the first slip stitch, insert the hook through the second chain stitch (counting from the hook). There should be only one strand of the chain stitch on the hook.

1st chain stitch
2nd chain stitch

2 Wrap the working yarn around the hook (yrh). Hold the start of the foundation chain in place with your left hand. Keep the yarn taut. With the hook pull the working yarn through the chain stitch in the direction of the arrow.

3 Work a slip stitch in all of the following chain stitches in the same way. Slip stitches should generally be worked quite loosely.

FASTENING OFF CHAINS & SLIP STITCHES

Stopping your crochet when it is complete is called "fastening off". As there is only one loop on your hook, the process is extremely simple. Here is a visual aid for how to fasten off a length of chains or a row of slip stitches.

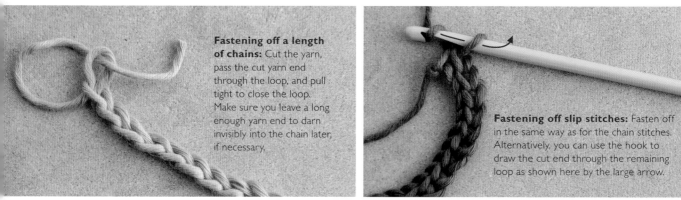

Fastening off a length of chains: Cut the yarn, pass the cut yarn end through the loop, and pull tight to close the loop. Make sure you leave a long enough yarn end to darn invisibly into the chain later, if necessary.

Fastening off slip stitches: Fasten off in the same way as for the chain stitches. Alternatively, you can use the hook to draw the cut end through the remaining loop as shown here by the large arrow.

PARTS OF STITCHES

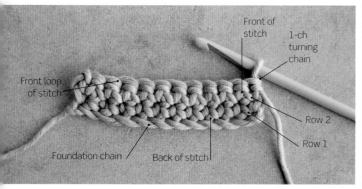

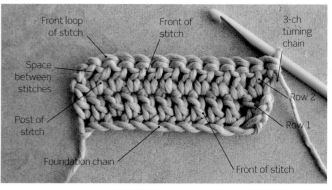

Double crochet stitches: Work two rows of double crochet and fasten off. Look closely at your sample and make sure you can identify all the parts of the stitch labelled above. If your crochet pattern tells you to work into the stitch below, always insert the hook under BOTH loops (the front loop and the back loop [not visible here from the front]) at the top of the stitch, unless it tells you to do otherwise.

Treble crochet stitches: Work two rows of treble crochet and fasten off. Again, make sure you can identify all the parts of the stitch labelled above. As for double crochet and all other crochet stitches, if your crochet pattern tells you to work into the stitch below, always insert the hook under both loops at the top of the stitch, unless it tells you to do otherwise.

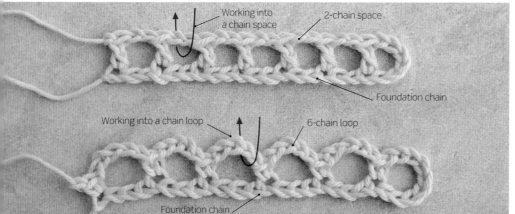

Chain spaces and chain loops: In many stitch patterns, chain stitches are introduced between basic stitches to create holes or spaces in the fabric. Spaces formed by short chains are called chain spaces, and those formed by long chains are called chain loops. When a crochet pattern instructs you to work into a chain space (or loop), always insert your hook from front to back through the space and not into the actual chain stitches.

DOUBLE CROCHET (abbreviation: dc)

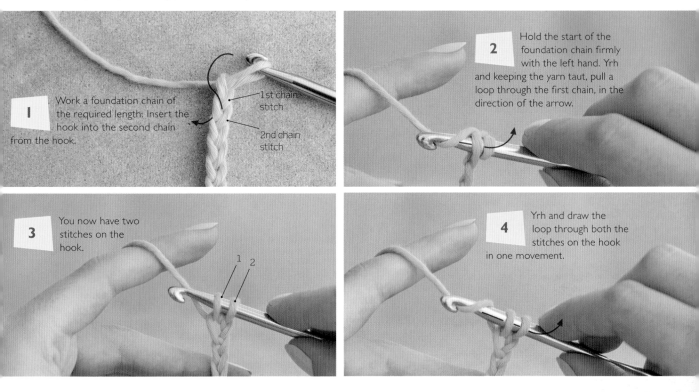

1 Work a foundation chain of the required length: Insert the hook into the second chain from the hook.

1st chain stitch

2nd chain stitch

2 Hold the start of the foundation chain firmly with the left hand. Yrh and keeping the yarn taut, pull a loop through the first chain, in the direction of the arrow.

3 You now have two stitches on the hook.

1 2

4 Yrh and draw the loop through both the stitches on the hook in one movement.

HALF TREBLE (abbreviation: htr)

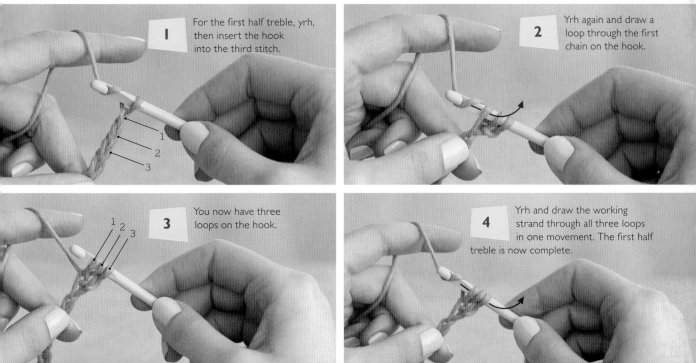

1 For the first half treble, yrh, then insert the hook into the third stitch.

1
2
3

2 Yrh again and draw a loop through the first chain on the hook.

3 You now have three loops on the hook.

1 2 3

4 Yrh and draw the working strand through all three loops in one movement. The first half treble is now complete.

TREBLE CROCHET (abbreviation: tr)

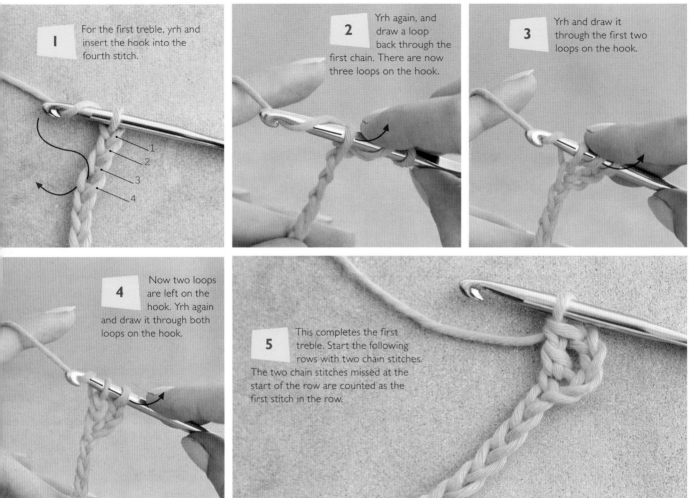

1 For the first treble, yrh and insert the hook into the fourth stitch.

2 Yrh again, and draw a loop back through the first chain. There are now three loops on the hook.

3 Yrh and draw it through the first two loops on the hook.

4 Now two loops are left on the hook. Yrh again and draw it through both loops on the hook.

5 This completes the first treble. Start the following rows with two chain stitches. The two chain stitches missed at the start of the row are counted as the first stitch in the row.

DOUBLE CROCHET DECREASE (abbreviation: 2dctog)

1 To decrease one stitch at the beginning of a row of double crochet, work up to the last yrh of the first dc in the usual way, but do not complete the stitch – there are now two loops on the hook. Insert the hook through the next stitch and draw a loop through.

1st incomplete double crochet

2 There are now three loops on the hook. Yrh and draw it through all three loops at once. This completes the decrease – where there were two stitches there is now only one.

2nd incomplete double crochet

HALF TREBLE DECREASE (abbreviation: 2htr tog)

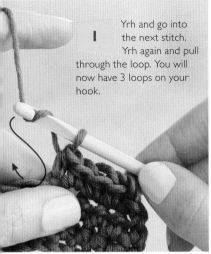

1 Yrh and go into the next stitch. Yrh again and pull through the loop. You will now have 3 loops on your hook.

2 Yrh and go into the next stitch. Yrh again and pull through the loop. You will now have 5 loops on your hook.

3 Yrh and pull through all 5 loops on the hook, in one movement, to complete the decrease.

CIRCLES & RINGS

CLOSING CHAIN STITCHES INTO A RING

Slip stitches are used to close a ring for working in the round. Work the required number of chain stitches, then insert the hook into the first chain stitch. Yrh, then pull the loop through both the stitches on the hook.

MAKING A MAGIC, ADJUSTABLE RING

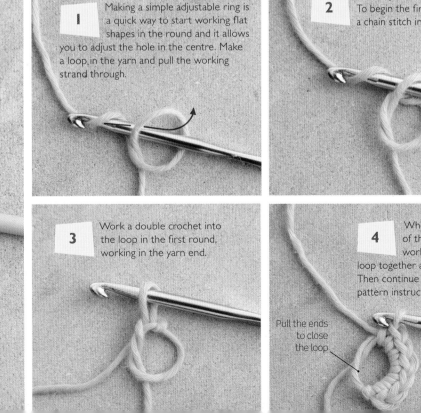

1 Making a simple adjustable ring is a quick way to start working flat shapes in the round and it allows you to adjust the hole in the centre. Make a loop in the yarn and pull the working strand through.

2 Do not pull the loop closed. To begin the first round, work a chain stitch in the loop.

3 Work a double crochet into the loop in the first round, working in the yarn end.

4 When every stitch of the first round is worked, pull the loop together at the yarn end. Then continue to follow the pattern instructions.

Pull the ends to close the loop

FLAT CIRCLES

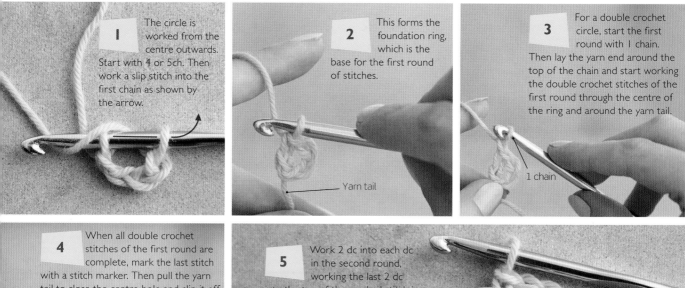

1 The circle is worked from the centre outwards. Start with 4 or 5ch. Then work a slip stitch into the first chain as shown by the arrow.

2 This forms the foundation ring, which is the base for the first round of stitches.

Yarn tail

3 For a double crochet circle, start the first round with 1 chain. Then lay the yarn end around the top of the chain and start working the double crochet stitches of the first round through the centre of the ring and around the yarn tail.

1 chain

4 When all double crochet stitches of the first round are complete, mark the last stitch with a stitch marker. Then pull the yarn tail to close the centre hole and clip it off close to the crochet.

Safety pin stitch marker

5 Work 2 dc into each dc in the second round, working the last 2 dc into the top of the marked stitch in the last round. Then count your stitches. Continue the pattern until the circle is the required size.

Move marker to last stitch at end of every round

Work stitches over yarn tail

BOBBLES

1 Bobbles are usually made with 3, 4, or 5 trebles. To work a 5-tr bobble, work 5 incomplete trebles into the same stitch. There are now 6 loops on the hook.

1 2 3 4 5 6

2 Yrh and draw a loop through all 6 loops on the hook.

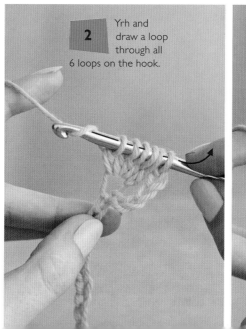

3 This completes all of the trebles at the same time and joins them at the top. Some bobbles are completed with an extra chain, as shown below by the arrow. Bobbles made with half trebles are called puff stitches.

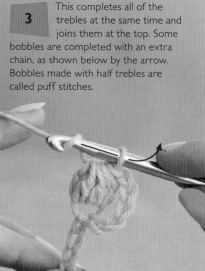

WORKING INTO THE BACK LOOP

Ridge effect: Working into only the back loops of the stitches in every row of double crochet creates a deep, ridged effect. The ridges are formed by the unworked loops.

WORKING INTO THE FRONT LOOP

Smooth effect: Working into only the front loop of each double crochet in the row below, on every row, creates a less pronounced texture than working into only the back loop.

WORKING INTO SPACES BETWEEN STITCHES

Treble space: Another way to achieve a subtly different texture with basic stitches is to work the stitches into the spaces between the stitches in the row below, instead of into the tops of the stitches.

WORKING INTO A CHAIN SPACE

Simple texture: Tweed stitch illustrates the simplest of all textures created by working into a chain space. Here, double crochet stitches are worked in the 1-chain spaces between the stitches in the row below, instead of into the tops of the stitches.

DOUBLE CROCHET EDGING

Top

Along top or bottom: To work a double crochet edging along the top or bottom of a piece of crochet, joining the yarn to the first stitch with a slip stitch, work 1ch, 1dc in the same place as the slip stitch, then work 1dc in each stitch below all along the edge.

Edge

Along row-ends: This is worked the same way, but it is not as easy to achieve an even edging. Experiment with how many stitches to work. If the finished edge looks flared, try working fewer stitches; and if it looks puckered, try working more.

FINISHING & SEAMS

WHEN YOU'VE FINISHED you will need to darn in ends, sew up seams, and block. Below is a handy reference for common finishing techniques. Always read the label on your yarn for any blocking instructions.

WET BLOCKING

If your yarn allows, wet blocking is the best way to even out your knitting. Using lukewarm water, either wash the piece or simply wet it. Squeeze and lay it flat on a towel, then roll the towel to squeeze out more moisture. Pin the piece into shape on layers of dry towels covered with a sheet. Leave to dry, then remove the pins.

STEAM BLOCKING

Only steam block if your yarn allows. Pin the piece to the correct shape, then place a clean damp cloth on top. Use a warm iron to create steam, barely touching the cloth. Do not rest the iron on the knitting. Avoid any garter stitch or ribbed areas. Before removing the pins, let the piece dry completely.

DARNING IN AN END

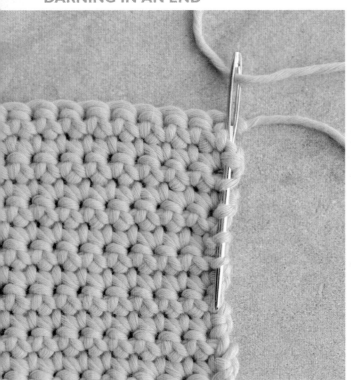

EDGE-TO-EDGE SEAM

Freshly completed work will have at least two yarn ends dangling from it – one at the start and one at the finish. Thread each end separately onto a blunt-ended needle and weave it vertically or horizontally through the stitches on the wrong side of work.

This seam is suitable for most patterns. To start, align the pieces of work with the wrong sides facing you. Work each stitch of the seam through the little pips formed along the edges as shown.

MATTRESS STITCH

I   **Mattress stitch** is practically invisible and is the best seam technique for ribbing and stocking stitch. Start by aligning the edges of the pieces to be seamed with both the right sides facing you.

2   **Insert the needle** from the front through the centre of the first knit stitch on one piece of knitting and up through centre of the stitch two rows above. Repeat on the other piece, working up the seam and pulling the edges together.

BACKSTITCH SEAM

OVERCAST SEAM

Align the pieces with the right sides together. Make one stitch forwards, and one stitch back into the starting point of the previous stitch as shown. Work the stitches as close to the edge of the work as possible. Backstitch can be used for almost any seam but is not suitable for super-bulky yarns.

With the right sides together, insert the needle from back to front through both layers, working through the centres of the edge stitches. Make each stitch in the same way. This seam is also called an Oversewn seam or a Whipped stitch seam.

ATTACHING PRESS STUDS

I   Make a knot and sew in end of thread, catching only half of each strand of yarn so that stitches don't go through to right side. Place stud in position centrally and insert needle inwards through surface of yarn near a stud hole just below the stud edge, then bring it up through the stud hole.

2   Repeat this three or four times through each hole, never taking the needle through to the right side. Move needle to next hole and repeat. To secure thread, sew two small backstitches, then sew a loop, thread the needle back through and pull tightly to secure thread.

The male side of the stud goes on the inside of the outer of a garment. Decide position of studs. Measuring can be inaccurate; count exact stitches and rows on each piece and mark positions with contrast thread.

INDEX

ACKNOWLEDGEMENTS

DK would like to thank the following people and companies for their valuable input, time, and dedication:

Pattern designers Caroline Birkett, Ruth Bridgeman, Ali Campbell, Susie Johns, Glenda Fisher, Fiona Goble, Zoe Halstead, Claire Montgomerie & Liz Ward

Technical consultant Susie Johns
Pattern checker Carol Ibbetson
Proofreader Angela Baynham
Photography assistant Julie Stewart
Editorial assistance Anne Hildyard & Toby Mann
Location house loan Sarah Mann
Prop hire Backgrounds Prop Hire

Modelling agency NEVS
Models Karolina Conchet; Custard the cat; Esme, Kit & Ted Daley; Teagan Dudley; Sarah Edwards; Colum Ewart; Tyro Heath; Chris Kelleher; Tilly Lee; Dani & Stewart Payne; Maria Thompson; Oliver Twelftret; & Walter the dog